500
ICT
TIPS
for
PRIMARY
TEACHERS

500 Tips from Kogan Page

500

ICT
TIPS
for
PRIMARY
TEACHERS

STEVE HIGGINS,
NICK PACKARD
& PHIL RACE

**KOGAN
PAGE**

London • Sterling (USA)

First published in 1999

Kogan Page Limited
120 Pentonville Road
London N1 9JN, UK
and
Stylus Publishing Inc.
22883 Quicksilver Drive
Sterling, VA 20166, USA

British Library Cataloguing in Publication Data

A CIP record for this book is available from the British Library.

ISBN 0 7494 2863 5

Typeset by Jo Brereton, Primary Focus, Haslington, Cheshire
Printed and bound in the UK by Biddles Ltd, Guildford and Kings Lynn

Contents

Key to Icons

Throughout the book, some tips have icons printed beside them. These icons are intended to help you locate relevant information more quickly, and therefore to ignore irrelevant ideas too. They are also intended to help make the meaning and focus of each tip a little clearer. The icons mean...

  Tip is particularly relevant for Early Years.

  Tip is particularly relevant for Key Stage 1.

  Tip is particularly relevant for Key Stage 2.

  A Teaching Point, or something that might suggest one!

  A Time Saver. For life both in and out of the classroom.

  Our Top Tip. Hopefully the most useful tip on the page!

Introduction

In this book we offer practical suggestions to help you to get into using computers in primary schools. The content of the book is very much based on some of the particular developments which have happened in primary education in England and Wales, where there is a 'National Curriculum' for schools which includes Information Technology as a discrete subject. However, we trust that many of our suggestions will be equally relevant to other parts of the world, where similar conditions exist and where computers are being introduced into primary education in similar ways.

In Britain, the term Information Technology (IT) has recently evolved into Information and Communications Technologies (ICT). In this book we try to use ICT when talking about Information and Communications Technologies generally. When we use IT, it often refers more specifically to England and Wales National Curriculum for Information Technology. We have tried to be consistent in this inconsistency!

The emphasis now seems to be on getting 'connected' and making the best of the information and communications revolution of the late 20th and early 21st Century. We could say that we are seeing two separate and parallel revolutions. One is an information explosion, where the amount of available information on just about everything has increased dramatically, and the range of formats through which this information is available has expanded rapidly. The other is the communications revolution, whereby information of all sorts can be communicated locally, nationally and world-wide by ever more sophisticated electronic means, and with great speed and increasing reliability. Children who are now in primary schools will need to be able to survive and thrive in this new world of information and communications technologies. Already, many of the young of the human species are proving to be more able than most of their predecessors (including parents and teachers) at embracing the effects of this revolution.

In the UK, Government initiatives are driving hard to meet the newly emerging needs associated with the communications and information technology revolution. The Superhighways initiative has been superseded by the National Grid for Learning. It is envisaged that every pupil will have access to e-mail in the first decade of the third millennium. The Virtual Teachers Centre will offer speedy access to a wealth of curriculum resources to teachers. Some people seem to believe we will have computers instead of teachers in the near future. However, such predictions were made decades ago when the first teaching machines, and early forms of open and flexible learning, were introduced, and the value of human beings as resources to facilitate learning has never been eroded in practice and, indeed, has become enhanced.

Our aim in writing this book is to offer support, encouragement and practical ideas to teachers wishing to develop both their personal ICT skills and their teaching skills. Alternatively, to mix metaphors, we hope that some of the ideas in this book will help teachers and IT coordinators to 'get on the bike', or perhaps pedal a little faster, both in terms of tackling new skills and in trying out different approaches for using ICT in the classroom.

It isn't a book that is meant to be read from cover to cover. Elsewhere there is a wealth of scholarly, research-based material about the communications revolution, so in this book we make no attempt to develop arguments on the basis of educational theories, or to promote any one particular approach to addressing rapid change. Rather, we see this book as a 'dip in' text – a quick and accessible alternative source of advice and ideas – and a trigger to help you to take our ideas and develop them into better ones of your own. The suggestions in this book are based on the collective practical experience and accumulated wisdom, including about 15 years of coordinating IT in primary schools (SH and NP), and as much time helping staff to develop and improve their practice, as well as rather more years than any of us care to remember working (and often learning from our own struggling) in the field of ICT in general.

While the whole of this book is intended to be useful to primary teachers in general, Chapters 7, 8 and 9 are written for the particular benefit of those with the responsibility of IT coordinator in their schools. Chapter 10 on 'The Internet' is intended for everyone. Sometimes we repeat ourselves! As you will quickly notice, there are nearer 700 tips in this book than 500, so we trust that you will regard our repeats as being intended to be helpful, so that when a point is important, you can find it in whichever part of the book you are using.

We have also added six appendices to the book. Appendix 1: 'Jargon-busting ICT terms for education' is a table of definitions and explanations of some of the main terms and acronyms you are likely to meet. This table is not to be taken as definitive, and indeed you will spot entries that are intended mainly to make you smile at times! Appendix 2: 'Audit your own ICT skills with quick quiz!' may make you feel better (or worse!). Appendix 3 lists 'Top 20 web sites', but of course this reflects our own opinions, and is current at the time of writing the book. However, we hope you will find them as useful starting points to lead you towards the sites that will prove most helpful to you. Appendix 4: 'Starting points for software' lists some details of suppliers and further web sites. Once more, just treat these as starting points. Likewise, Appendix 5: 'Some British educational acronyms and abbreviations' collects together some of the terms and phrases that are in everyday use in primary schools in England and Wales, but which may need translating for readers for other parts of Britain or the world. We could not resist reflecting in our 'definitions' of some of these terms several of the more popular feelings that primary teachers we know have about them. Appendix 6: 'Further reading'. There is a great deal of information around now, and the most important thing is to seek and find information that you find useful and appropriate for your own needs, and for those of your pupils.

At times, the style of this book is certainly somewhat tongue in cheek! It is definitely intended to be on the side of the teachers, who may sometimes feel that the world is conspiring to make more difficult their mission of helping primary children to learn and develop. However if the tone of our book helps to make the absurd amount of jargon bandied around in the area of ICT more understandable through gentle irony, then so much the better! We hope that most of the wry smiles that it may engender will be accompanied by useful learning points.

Finally, in this age of technology, we don't want to stop just because the book is now in print. We have included details of the address of a web site that we are setting up to get feedback from *you*. If you have comments, criticism or suggestions for the next edition of this book, contact us via this web site, where we hope to maintain the momentum of sharing yet more practical suggestions on the use of ICT in primary education.

Steve Higgins
Nick Packard
Phil Race

December 1998

Chapter 1   Coping with ICT in the Classroom

There are a great many problems associated with teaching Information and Communications Technology in schools. This is especially true in primary classrooms where children require high levels of support and structure to facilitate learning. In addition, so often at present there is only one computer, limited software and limited time actually to teach the skills needed to use the computer. As a result, in many primary classrooms, ICT is reduced to a 'choosing activity' for much of the time. This picture is likely to change very rapidly in the next decade or two but, meanwhile, we offer practical suggestions to help you to make the most of the facilities that you already may have.

In this chapter we offer practical support and ideas for managing and teaching IT effectively and, subsequently, for getting the best out of the time and the equipment available. We have divided our suggestions into the following sections.

1   Setting up an IT area
2   Getting to grips with hardware and software
3   Managing IT work in the classroom
4   Developing self-supporting activities
5   Effective use of support materials
6   Planning appropriate activities for ICT

1

Setting up an IT area

It is important that you make the best of the equipment and resources that you have. There is usually more equipment and software around than is used, and it is worth reflecting on how you can use what you have got more effectively.

1   **Pick a practical space.** If you are setting up a discrete area for IT in a classroom, try to make it self-contained, make sure it is near a mains socket and that it will not distract others. If you are putting a cluster of computers together, try to ensure they are accessible. Aim to make sure children can be left there on their own, but can still be seen (in a wider corridor or in a very central classroom). If possible, make the area chosen close to the IT coordinator's room.

2   **Make sure you can set up a whole class demonstration to introduce new software.** It is very inefficient to teach 16 pairs of pupils to do the same thing 16 times. A brief demonstration to the whole class is more effective, even if it means moving the computer for a session to a different place in the classroom by using a long extension cable, so that all the pupils can see the demonstration clearly.

3   **Make sure the computer does not face a window.** Firstly, direct sunlight on the computer might damage it, or floppy disks. Secondly, more importantly, the glare of the sun on the screen might make it very difficult for children to use. Similarly, make sure chairs and screens are the correct height for good posture.

4   **Put things the children don't need out of the way.** While you want to encourage children to develop an understanding of how all this stuff works, we have all heard stories of what can get pushed into floppy disk slots or seen what an enthusiastic four-year-old can do to a diskette! As far as possible, keep the things the children don't need to know about just yet firmly stowed out of sight. Some software only needs a mouse, especially for early years children, so even the keyboard can be hidden away.

5   **Make sure children have access to resources they do need.** Putting work cards, help sheets, overlays and reference CD-ROMs for older children, or even a new telephone socket for Internet access, near to the computer, will help to promote more independent work.

6   **Try to put your computer area where there is good access to display space.** If you are setting up one or maybe two computers in a particular area in your classroom, make sure the displays of pupils' IT work can go next to the computer itself. You could also display prompts or hints to aid independent use.

7   **Use what you have got.** IT in the National Curriculum involves computers, calculators, programmable robots and a whole host of other electronic devices. It's not all high tech, however. Some aspects of the National Curriculum require you to consider wider uses and applications of IT, work that in itself may not involve technology more complex than a paper and pencil.

8   **Investigate what the software you *have* got can do.** Most programs have added features that regular users, and even very experienced users, know nothing about. Some handbooks give a good overview of the capabilities of the software by way of introduction and are worth reading. A flick through the handbook can sometimes point you to new possibilities, too. Remember, though, that handbooks are rarely designed to be read one page at a time and are more suitable for dipping into.

9   **Decide what more you need *now*.** There will be areas of the IT curriculum where you do not have enough equipment, effective programs for what you need or an adequate range of software or hardware (eg, better database program, concept keyboard, programmable robot). Find out urgently what you really need, and make suggestions about how the school could afford to buy it or acquire it.

10   **Nag the headteacher/IT coordinator.** This might be about making the computer secure and permanently in place where you want it in the classroom. Do this to save time spent every day setting up the machines – a major time waster!

11   **Beg, borrow or rescue extra equipment.** Redundant equipment may not offer all the possibilities of the latest Internet-ready multimedia machine. However, many of the skills in the National Curriculum for IT can be developed with older equipment, helping you to make the most of the newer equipment.

12   **Don't go overboard, blinding your pupils with technology.** Make *good* use of a limited range of software and equipment. We suggest one main program per half term for the year group you are teaching. You might have other favourite 'time-fillers' you wish to use from time to time, but do not be fooled into thinking these will help you to develop pupils' IT capability as required in the National Curriculum.

13   **Borrow extra computers or equipment.** Arrange a loan for half a term when you want to focus on developing specific skills, or for an afternoon on a regular basis when another class cannot use it. Many primary schools are now organizing clusters of machines, so that teachers can focus on teaching with them rather than using them as occupiers (albeit worthy ones) for a couple of pupils at a time. Your local IT centre may have extra programmable robots, or arrange a loan and swap with another school so you can teach the skills of using them more efficiently.

14   **Establish your systems.** How much will pupils be responsible for? Can you get basic prompt cards for routine procedures, such as 'Switching On', 'Loading Software', 'Saving Files', 'Printing', and so on?

15   **Get support.** You should not be attempting to join the ICT revolution as a solitary soldier. There should be systems in place in school for learning about the hardware and help sheets for software for teachers, if not for the pupils. Someone, somewhere will have made resources like this, and your local teachers' centre should be able to provide some. The difficult question is – will it be easier to go out and look for the resources or to create them for yourself? (See Appendix 3 for some suggestions.)

2

Getting to grips with hardware and software

There is never enough time to do this properly, but that does not mean that it is OK to ignore the whole issue. Even computer gurus will only be experts in a small area of educational ICT use. The secret is to start by doing a *little*, and doing it regularly, then accepting that you will keep up to date with *some* of what is available.

1   **Borrow the class computer for a holiday.** (*Not* Christmas!) Try to learn *one* new program for use after the holiday. Borrow some children (if you do not have any of the appropriate age) to try out what you have learnt, or so that you can get them to teach you what to do.

2   **Get some staff training.** Over the next few of years in the UK there will be hundreds of millions of pounds spent on ICT training for teachers. Think about what your needs are (you could try the Self-assessment and Needs Analysis Quiz at the back of this book), and try to make sure you get your share of the training on offer, and that what you get matches what *you* need to learn.

3   **Just have a go!** Adults, in general, are more reluctant than children to try (**TT**) things out with computers, in case they get it 'wrong'. Learning from mistakes is often the quickest way to get into new computer software. You will not be able to learn effectively unless you play about and try things out.

4   **Be clear about what you want your pupils to learn.** Identify how you expect their IT capability (in National Curriculum speak) to be developed with the software you have. Then learn how to use just those particular applications. Your school's scheme of work may help here.

5   **Use a backup program.** Make sure you have a backup of each program in school and that you are not using the original disks. Companies which have found ways to prevent copying of disks will usually supply new disks on receipt of any corrupted ones you send them.

6   **Try out programs as you would expect a pupil to.** Find out what happens when you deliberately do something wrong. It will help you to rescue pupils who get stuck when working in the classroom. You may also find features of programs you did not know about. Some programs offer good help on screen, too.

7   **Ask for a student teacher who is good at ICT.** Teacher training institutions must ensure that their students are fully trained in ICT. They should also have access to good quality resources and support. Most of them work in partnership with local schools and they can be a valuable source of help. This will not only help you to keep your knowledge up to date, but will be a chance for your pupils to learn from someone else.

8   **Get your own computer.** This is not a cheap option, but you will need practice at using technology if you wish to develop your own skills. There is no quick route to becoming an ICT expert. Ideally, get the same sort of machine that you will be using in the classroom, so you will be learning skills and procedures which will help you to teach. However, it will also be useful in other areas of teaching if your own machine can perform other tasks, such as reasonable quality desktop publishing if you want to use it to produce resources. Alternatively, you might want to consider how you will get access to the Internet. Some primary schools are now using presentation packages for teachers, so that they can do demonstrations to a whole class with a projector connected to a laptop computer.

9   **Learn to use effective programs.** These are ones which can be used in more than one situation, or which can support a range of tasks and abilities, rather than one which has a limited use. The types of applications which may be suitable include a word processor suitable for the age you teach, a graphing program or a spreadsheet program for Key Stage 2, or a program around which you can develop a range of identified skills or activities.

10 **Find ways to keep up to date.** As computers have become more sophisticated so has the software that they run. This means that new programs tend to be more complex and take longer to learn than older ones. It is debatable whether the newer programs are always more effective at supporting learning! However, if you do not become familiar with newer software as it becomes available, you will have a bigger jump to

get up to date at a later stage. Your IT coordinator or local IT centre should be able to advise you on what to look at. The IT centre may have different versions of popular programs to try out, as may your local teacher training institution. Some companies also have an approval scheme for viewing software. Realistically, this might mean that you try to look at one new program a term.

3

Managing IT work in the classroom

There is no simple prescription for effective management in the classroom, and you will need to review what you do regularly as things change. The increasing emphasis on focused literacy and numeracy sessions is undoubtedly going to squeeze IT time in the short term. However, the targets for pupils' ICT use, especially for electronic mail (e-mail) and the World Wide Web (WWW), means it will have considerable emphasis, too. (In England and Wales, IT is also still in the Office for Standards in Education's (OFSTED's) gaze!)

1 **Use ICT resources as much as you can.** What you can achieve with ICT will depend upon how often, and for how long, pupils in your class have access to the technology. The more equipment or computers pupils have access to, the more time they will use them and the more they will be able to achieve.

2 **Use computers to teach and demonstrate.** It can be difficult to organize a classroom so that large groups of pupils can see the computer. However, it is efficient to introduce a new program to the whole class rather than repeating the introduction lots of times. Some ideas can be more easily demonstrated than explained. When using a word processor for demonstrations, try increasing the font size or the magnification (usually 'view %', for example), to explain 'copy' and 'paste' or to demonstrate sentence level work.

3 **Be critical.** Just because it is on the computer does not necessarily mean it is a good idea. Check that the software or particular activity is actually helping the pupils to achieve the learning outcome you want. Pupils quickly learn how to operate a program and may avoid reading any text on-screen, for example, unless they actually need to read it to progress to the next part of the program. Similarly, in maths drill and practice programs, many of them have an automated feedback prompt, or move pupils on after two or three incorrect responses. Some pupils quickly learn

that they can move on without doing much, so their apparent progress through a program may not indicate their real learning.

4   **Be flexible about borrowing and lending equipment.** To make the most of the hardware and equipment you have in school, share things around and organize your equipment to get the best from it. If a task really requires all of the floor robots or half a dozen computers, plan to borrow equipment from others and be prepared to lend whatever usually resides in your room!

5   **Decide the best place for the equipment.** In practice you will probably have little choice, but it is worth reconsidering your options. Could you have a computer in the school's TV room? You could then demonstrate programs to a whole class. A cable to connect a computer to TV or video monitor (called a display converter) is relatively cheap and might allow you to organize a whole class teaching session once a week. Pupils could even present their work this way – the impact on them of seeing their work on a large TV screen is considerable.

6   **Maximize the time that computers are in use.** Resources are expensive and it is difficult to plan for ICT equipment to be in use all the time. Can you provide access at break times or lunch times? What about before and after school? Are there other adults or older children you could get to help out? Can you use Mrs Cummerbund's computer while her class are doing PE?

7   **What about the summer term?** Could you reorganize the resources for the summer term, so that classes which are not delighting in national assessment tests could get best use of the equipment in school?

8   **Involve the children in the management of the computers.** You could train pupils to be responsible for switching on and shutting down at the beginning or end of the day whenever possible – even the youngest children are easily able to do this! Pupils usually take this sort of responsibility very seriously.

9   **Limit your objectives to what is achievable.** Try setting up a record of who used which program on which day, so that the record is completed by the pupils themselves. You can then concentrate on assessing and recording their IT capability (see Chapter 6).

10 **Don't show your frustration when the equipment goes wrong.** Some pupils will assume that you are cross with them, particularly young children. If a computer does not do what you expect, either someone has made a mistake, or it is faulty. Pupils, particularly young children, very rarely make deliberate mistakes. If it is faulty, it is not your or the child's fault.

4

Developing self-supporting activities

You need time to teach a group effectively and, therefore, you need to ensure you are not always leaping across the classroom to sort out problems on the computer. However, you also need to make sure that the pupils working on the computer do not teach each other incorrectly – pupil-to-pupil instructions can all too easily become a cascade of misleading whispers!

1   **Keep it simple.** It is easy to make a supposedly self-supporting activity too complicated by bombarding the pupils with information. Plan for one step at a time!

2   **Keep in step.** If your school has a detailed scheme of work for IT, make sure that what you do follows on from what the children should have done last year, and leads nicely into what they will be doing next year. The easiest way to ensure children can work independently is to make sure they are working at an appropriate level.

3   **Introduce the activity to the whole class.** If this is not feasible, then at least introduce it to a large group, with a demonstration at the computer. It may be possible to organize a demonstration at the end of the morning by getting pupils to help move furniture so that they can all see. A bribe of 'only *sensible* children will be helping me to demonstrate what to do' usually works!

4   **Use support cards.** Try using information cards, prompts, wall charts, step-by-step instructions, and so on. Don't forget to prepare these on a computer, and keep a copy on disk, so that they are easier to replace when they become too chewed, glued or printed over by mistake. Older pupils can even help to write them as they become more familiar with software. The language coordinator will love this idea!

5   **Teach others to give support**. This can include other pupils in the class, older pupils as well as adult helpers. It takes longer in the beginning, but it pays off in the long run. Some primary schools have a coordinated program of teaching adult volunteers, who have their voluntary work accredited to lead on to further training for them.

6   **Train pupils in a system.** For example, plan for pupils to have the responsibility to go and get the person whose turn it is next. This might be by using a list of names as a sign-up sheet, or allowing a set time with a kitchen timer, or a set number of problems on screen, and making them responsible for helping the next pupil or pair of pupils. Don't forget that such systems need monitoring as, 'Oh, Miss, I was just helping like you asked!' can seem an excellent work avoidance strategy!

7   **Give the pupils time to play.** When we learn something new we all need time to explore and find out what it can do. You might consider letting pupils have a go at break or lunch time to play with new software before setting them tasks to do. They may even learn things you don't know about!

8   **Change the groupings of the pupils at the computer.** Have more experienced pupils work with less experienced ones, but make sure they understand *how* to take turns or share the work in the particular context of the program they are using. For example, prescribe a set number of screens per pupil, or make one child responsible for putting full stops in a piece of writing correctly.

9   **Make sure no one dominates.** It is worth making sure that a range of pupils become the 'experts' and that your experts know how to *explain* what to do, rather than just do it for others. 'Helen, fold your arms and *tell* them what to do' helps the others to learn, and Helen herself to learn even more than if she just does something she already knows how to do.

10   **Make sure the pupils are clear about *what* they have got to do and *why* they are doing it.** Ask them now and again why they are doing things, and what exactly they are trying to do. When pupils know what they are supposed to be learning from a task and why, they are much more likely to learn effectively and productively.

11   **Be explicit about where pupils are to get support from.** Explain to them when they are *intended* to use prompt cards, other (specified) pupils, or an adult, or yourself.

12   **Review each activity with the whole class.** Preferably do this at the computer. Review what some successful pupils have done, so as to give others a clear picture of what they have to try to do when it is their turn.

5

Effective use of support materials

Pupils will learn how to get support from the easiest source possible. If you always leap across and sort the computer out they will always nag you to help. But, if their turn with the machine ends when they get stuck, it can be a great incentive for them to learn how to do it correctly! The following suggestions may help you to make your pupils more self-sufficient in their usage of computers.

1   **Tell them *when* they get it right.** Make sure pupils use the support which is available, praise them publicly when they do. There is a tendency in education (and in life in general) to be quick to tell people when they've got something wrong, and not to mention everything that they've got right.

2   **Tell them *why* they got it right.** Pupils learn much more quickly when they understand why they did something well. Other pupils also pick up what it is you are looking for.

3   **Make sure the easiest way to get support is the way you want them to get it.** Make it easier for them to use the support you provide than simply to ask you (unless you are supporting that particular activity). If you usually leap enthusiastically across the classroom to show them how to do something they will continue to pester you. Pupils will always take the easiest option – don't always be that!

4   **Use prompt cards and help sheets.** Especially use those that the children have helped to write or refine. Simple cards with 'Save' or 'Print' instructions can help remind pupils of what to do when they get stuck. Laminating cards and sheets can increase their life and can protect them from being written upon. Clear plastic envelopes are almost as good.

5 **Keep written instructions brief and use pictures, if possible.** Many

manuals (if you've got one!) or guides, have illustrations you could
photocopy. It is also relatively easy on most computers to take a snapshot
of the screen and clip out the relevant tool bar, window or menu.
Sometimes you can print out a screen dump, and cut and paste sections
of this into instruction sheets.

6 **Train pupils to use on-screen help where it is available.** Decide first
whether the on-screen help is, of course, useful. Try to use it yourself
first, then point the children in the right direction. Text-to-speech can make
writing easier to read by providing prompts. Many CD-ROMs and word
processors have this facility.

7 **Use support materials provided by the program.** Many have step-by-
step instructions, along the lines 'Getting Going' or 'Quick Setup', as
provided by the manufacturer. Most of these are easily simplified! Some
can even be used by pupils directly. This may be something to consider
when buying new programs.

8 **Support computer tasks with other activities that can be done away
from the computer.** By doing this, some of the motivation and enthusiasm
spills over into other tasks, and it can be a good way of linking ideas and
skills, so pupils practise them in another situation.

9 **Share your support materials.** Other teachers will be more likely to swap
theirs, too! It can be useful to have several different kinds of support
materials, and to find which works best for different pupils, and maybe
to differentiate the level of support to match pupils' abilities to use it.

10 **Keep copies of everything you do.** Whether hard or soft copy, it won't
last forever. It is quicker to photocopy a master kept in a plastic wallet
than print out a new one from a file. If you think you might want to change
it, however, an electronic copy is also essential.

6

Planning appropriate activities for ICT

Don't reinvent the wheel! There is a lot of published material available about planning for IT. In the UK, your Local Education Authority (LEA) should have resources to share. Other teachers in your school and beyond will have prepared and planned, too. The following suggestions could help you to learn from others' experience.

1   **Use the National Curriculum IT program of study and your school's scheme of work (if available).** If you are lucky, you might have access to suggested programs and examples of planning from previous years. Very recently, the QCA published a Scheme of Work for IT in Key Stages 1 and 2, offering some good examples of how to cover the National Curriculum effectively.

2   **Find out what other teachers use working with the same age pupils and similar machines.** Sharing ideas and practical suggestions from other teachers is an excellent starting point. Find out what worked well, and ask where the problems were found to be.

3   **Get support from the LEA IT centre or advice from IT adviser.** They may already have teachers and pupils guides for the software you are using. The centre, or adviser, may be able to arrange visits to schools with similar resources to see what they do; they may even tailor training programs to help.

4   **Get materials from the National Grid for Learning.** In the UK, the British Educational Communications and Technology agency (BECTa) (http://becta.org.uk) – formerly the National Council for Educational Technology, NCET – produces suggestions, materials and ideas for the national grid for learning at (http:www.ngfl.gov.uk) and at the Virtual Teacher Centre (http://www.vtc.ngfl.gov.uk).

5   **Find out which programs the pupils have used before.** It is always best to begin with activities the pupils are familiar with at the start of the year, while you are establishing new routines and becoming familiar with the class.

6   **Plan a range of activities over the course of the year.** This might be with a specific focus for each half term. For example, it could be along the lines of: Half-term 1 – Wordprocessing; Half-term 2 – Graphics or drawing package (Christmas/Festivals artwork); Half-term 3 – Maths number; Half-term 4 – Maths shape and space or data handling; Half-term 5 – Combining pictures and text; Half-term 6 – Control/IT implications.

7   **Integrate the IT components into your main teaching aims.** This could be for a block of work where possible. Examples could include using a Roamer for work on estimation in maths by setting the scale to appropriate units for your pupils, or planning a redrafting activity on the computer to support the sentence or text level work you are doing in English.

8   **Use the computer for direct teaching, too.** Often a computer activity can be completed by pupils alongside class work. Could you use the computer with a group where you redraft some prepared writing as an introduction for them to complete a paper and pencil exercise?

9   **Do not get pupils to copy type finished work into a neat version**. It is a waste of the computer's time. It is also a waste of the pupils' time. It is much more valuable for pupils to use the computer to redraft and make changes to their work, than laboriously key in their handwritten story, particularly for children who are struggling with keyboard skills anyway. If typing skills are the issue, set up a lunch time club with a typing tutor program.

10 **Be realistic about how long activities will take.** If everyone is to get a 'turn' doing the same thing it will take a *long* time for a class of 30 pupils. Consider whether they could do variations on a task which focuses on the same skills, and which can be made into a class book for example.

Chapter 2   IT as a Discrete Subject

Despite the fact that the England and Wales National Curriculum takes great pains to stress the cross-curricular nature of IT, it is important to think of IT as a subject in its own right, too. If not, it becomes extremely difficult to ensure that children make progress in IT, and it becomes almost impossible to focus on what IT skills you are trying to teach. In this situation, progress in IT may still happen, but which skills are developed and how far those skills are stretched is simply left to chance – a situation OFSTED inspectors could get their teeth into!

In this chapter, we will consider the sorts of IT-related skills teachers might be looking to develop, and the sorts of activities they might use to try to develop them. These ideas will be focused particularly on the needs of the class teacher, whereas Chapter 7 on 'Managing IT in Primary Schools' covers some similar ideas, but focused more on the needs of the IT coordinators and school's management.

Our suggestions are grouped under these headings.

7   Why consider IT as a discrete subject?
8   What should I teach in IT?
9   Covering the National Curriculum
10   Integrating IT with the curriculum
11   Planning for continuity in IT

7

Why consider IT as a discrete subject?

Language skills are applicable across subject areas. We often think of the sorts of language we might develop in maths, science, humanities, and so on. Some ICT skills are applicable across subject areas, too, but those skills may also need to be identified in terms of the IT curriculum. Here are some reasons why you might want to consider ICT and IT separately.

1 **Because you have to.** It is a statutory part of the curriculum and will be inspected. Formal assessment of IT capabilities is firmly on the agenda, and with the government committing so much money to the development of ICT in education, it will want proof that our money has not been wasted.

2 **Because you need to teach IT actively.** It is no good expecting children just to acquire skills. As long as they have access to resources they will acquire skills, and probably almost as quickly as they might if you were teaching them. But you need to raise their awareness of what ICT can do. You need to extend their technological vocabulary in order to ensure they can be taught in the future, and you need to help them to put their skills in context. With the onset of the 'digital revolution', talk is going to be even more important, because the personal computer is still a very long way from being able to enter into any kind of meaningful dialogue.

3 **Because you have to try to ensure continuity**. Especially if your school has quite a detailed scheme of work, you need to make sure that you have fulfilled your side of the bargain.

4 **Because you have to ensure progression.** If you don't teach it, how can you be sure that it will get any better? If it's not formally on the agenda, it could remain as an optional extra in people's vision.

5   **Because OFSTED will expect to see it.** The recent revision in the inspection framework has increased OFSTED's beady glare in this area. They will want to see evidence that IT skills are being taught, not simply absorbed by osmosis.

6   **Because it is a national priority.** A lot of money is being spent on ICT, and you need to make sure that your pupils and your school don't miss out.

7   **Because pupils are motivated by ICT.** The majority of pupils enjoy using ICT, particularly computers, and are therefore keen to engage in the learning tasks that computers offer.

8   **Because ICT is effective.** Identifying where ICT has the potential to make a significant difference to pupils' learning is therefore vital.

9   **Because ICT is useful.** ICT has had a tremendous impact on the world outside school. Many pupils will continue to use ICT well beyond their schooldays. There are ways it can be beneficial in school, too!

10 **Because you can have the computer in use all day every day and still not be doing IT.** IT in the National Curriculum is about the pupils *themselves* using ICT in their learning. Try working out where a spelling practice program fits in to the programme of study!

11 **Because if you think of IT just as a subject, you won't do it justice!** IT is primarily a tool for teaching and learning across the curriculum. Although there are specific skills in ICT, they need to be delivered through some content. It makes sense to ensure that the content is linked to other work the pupils are doing.

8

What should I teach in IT?

What you need to teach will usually depend upon the age of the pupils, their previous computer experience, the appropriate part of the programs of study in the National Curriculum for IT, your school's scheme of work for IT and the particular focus of work in your classroom at the time. The following suggestions may trigger your own thoughts on how and when to teach using IT.

1   **Teach skills that can be used across the curriculum.** Many aspects of the ICT skills that pupils learn should have a more general application. It is pointless teaching them how to use a complex package, which is difficult to use, no matter how much of a computer wizard *you* are. It is very likely that an easier one will soon be available.

2   **Teach basic word processing skills.** Pupils need to be taught about things like word-wrap (when the computer moves a word on to the following line automatically), the return key, when to use the shift and not the Caps Lock keys, and similar everyday word processing skills. Bad habits may not make much difference in the early days, but they can make a huge difference by the time the children are reaching the end of their primary education.

3   **Progress to more complex skills.** Pupils need to be taught both *how* and *when* to use cut and paste, for example. It would be silly to try to teach them these skills while they are still struggling to build simple sentences.

4   **Consider getting a typing tutor program to develop keyboard skills**. This could be for regular, brief practice at the beginning of a longer IT session, if you have lots of computers, or as part of a lunch time club. Although you might believe that typing may be set to become a thing of the past, with voice input on its way, don't bank on it! Voice recognition software has now been available (and working) for a long time, but more and more people still need to use keyboards.

5 **Combining words and pictures is a good place to begin.** This could be basic, factual writing with some clip art. From here, the pupils can easily progress to creating their own pictures and deciding on fonts and layout in an integrated or desktop publishing package.

6 **Teach pupils how to use a toolbox or palette program.** Most drawing and painting programs use this approach. A window, or bar, contains tools like a pencil or circle shape for pupils to choose to make a drawing. It is essential that you teach pupils how to select and alter the tools they choose for drawing and painting. Using a rectangle tool to draw a house outline is more efficient (and pleasing) than using a freehand tool or building it up with a series of straight lines. A whole class demo is an efficient way of showing pupils the advantages of the appropriate tools.

7 **A calculator is a good way to explain a spreadsheet.** The formula you put in a cell is the same as a series of key presses on the computer. Spreadsheets can therefore be seen as a whole series of linked calculators. Unless pupils understand the different ways in which a cell can be used, they will not appreciate the possibilities in a spreadsheet. They will simply use it as a grid and not see it as hundreds of little calculator boxes.

8 **Teach pupils, at least once, about a database that is *not* on the computer.** It can be difficult for pupils to get a picture of what a database is and how it works. Children will have no experience of a card index system, and they should be given an opportunity to develop their understanding of a database at some point. This does not have to be before they use a database on a computer, but could usefully be done at the same time. This way they can also consider the advantages and disadvantages of using the computer as a tool in this context.

9 **Teach analysis and interrogation of databases and charts, too.** Children often enter data and create graphs and charts, although they are rarely taught how to ask appropriate questions and how to find answers from them. In later life, they are likely to spend more time on working with existing databases than on creating new ones.

10 **Remember to review ICT work with the children.** It is often revealing to ask children questions about what they have learnt, or to get them to ask questions of each other. You should discover all too accurately what they understand, and what has not yet clicked! Reviewing ICT work is often ignored at the end of a lesson, because the whole activity can continue for a number of days.

9

Covering the National Curriculum

The National Curriculum requirements for IT are demanding in themselves, even without adding the capital C for Communications and considering e-mail and the WWW. The following suggestions may remind you of some of the main things to be covered.

1   **Remember that IT is a tool for pupils to use.** IT in the National Curriculum is about exploring and problem solving across the curriculum, and about helping children to understand how IT can be used to create, explore and solve these problems.

2   **Remember to make IT relevant.** IT in the National Curriculum is about relating it to their own lives. However, it is difficult to predict how we will be using ICT in five years' time when some of Year 6 children will be leaving school, let alone in more than 10 years' time when this year's Reception class will finish compulsory schooling.

3   **Remember that ICT is a powerful *communications* tool.** Communicating and handling information – text, graphs, pictures and sound – is a major strand of the National Curriculum and emphasizes IT as a tool for pupils.

4   **Combining text and pictures for a specific audience can be as easy as designing and making a card or a poster.** You would also need to get the pupils to evaluate the effectiveness or appropriateness of what they had done to achieve the learning objectives.

5   **The problem with using pie charts is that pupils think it is just a piece of cake!** Plotting graphs and adding text is easy with current programs. Interpreting this information and analysing it is not so straightforward. When the construction of graphs and charts is easy, the teaching emphasis

needs to be on interpreting and making connections to other areas of maths, particularly number. This way, visual information will reinforce and develop pupils' understanding of number.

6   **Analysing information is often missed out.** Pupils do not always need to go through the complete cycle (identify the problem, pose a question, evidence, data, evaluate, check solution). Pupils are not expected to organize a database from scratch until level 5.

7   **Identify a purpose for finding information.** Database and CD-ROM work is not just about printing vast sections of text and pretty pictures. Emphasize the value of information retrieval skills, and making searches purposeful and efficient.

8   **It is not as hard as you think.** Controlling, monitoring and modelling work needs good resources. If it is currently unmanageable you might need to reconsider your equipment or what you are trying to achieve. Helping children to learn to use a tape recorder, or to set the timer in a video player, or to program a microwave oven are all examples of control. Control work with Roamer, Pip or Pixie is hugely versatile: getting young children in Key Stage 1 to get it to draw a square, or to use it for non-standard measure can be absorbing and valuable; yet Year 6 pupils can become just as absorbed in planning escape routes involving measurement in centimetres and degrees by using the same piece of equipment.

9   **Remember your targets.** Your target is that by the end of the primary school all pupils can use and combine different forms of information, and show an awareness of audience. They add to, amend and interrogate information that has been stored. They understand the need for care in framing questions when collecting, accessing and interrogating information. Pupils interpret their findings, question plausibility and recognize that poor quality information yields unreliable results. Pupils use IT systems to control events in a predetermined manner, to sense physical data and to display it. They use IT-based models and simulations to explore patterns and relationships, and to make simple predictions about the consequences of their decision making. They compare their use of IT with other methods' (Level 4 level description).

10 **Get real!** The target quoted above means that pupils have to be able to achieve it in *real* situations. By the end of Year 6, your pupils should be using IT in the process of working on an open-ended task. This could be searching for information on a CD-ROM or on the WWW, and then presenting what they find with a desktop publishing package as part of a project (maybe producing a leaflet or poster). They should use databases

as a starting point when looking for possible answers to questions in history say, 'Why did the Spanish Armada set sail?' They should be able to cross-reference and compare what they find on a CD-ROM with what they find in a book. They should be able to enter data from a survey into a database or spreadsheet with care, compare results with others and look for reasons why their answers don't quite match. They should be able to make the decision to use a spreadsheet to record various measurements, for example, plotting distance against time in a scientific investigation. A scheme of work for IT should not only give children a range of experiences showing what IT can do, it should also help them to develop the necessary skills to decide when and how to use it in their work.

10

Integrating IT with the curriculum

ICT is only a tool. The content can be as varied as you need. It is, therefore, essential to consider how you can integrate it into your teaching, so it is effective both in developing pupils' IT capability and their skills, knowledge and understanding in different areas of the curriculum. Already in this chapter we have stressed the need to make usage of IT real and meaningful for pupils. The following suggestions may give you further ideas for integrating IT.

1   **Use IT to support other areas of your teaching.** It can help in finding and compiling resources for your teaching sessions. These can be ideas and activities for pupils to use away from the computer.

2   **Use whole class demonstrations to start pupils thinking.** A CD-ROM entry, or talking story book page, can be used as a discussion point with the whole class and can be an excellent starting point for further activities away from the computer.

3   **Use IT to support pupils' learning.** This is particularly relevant when working on group activities based around the computer. The computer can be used as a resource perhaps initially using a CD-ROM, and then as a focus for the presentation of the work using a word processor or desktop publishing package. Planning a time line of the Victorians in history, with pairs of pupils writing or illustrating a particular date, or an annotated map in geography, with individual pupils covering different aspects of a country, can both follow this type of organization.

4   **Combine the work different pupils do.** Unless you are very well supplied with computers, the amount of work pupils will be able to complete using a computer will be limited. However, assembling work into a collection (such as a class book on the various aspects of their study of the Egyptians

or a guide to using a computer-based simulation) enables IT work to be used as a resource by everyone while still producing a significant piece of work that everyone feels part of.

5   **Get the pupils to use slide shows and presentations.** They are easier than you might think, and are appropriate across the curriculum as a summary of a theme or unit of work. The slide show module on KidPix, for example, is remarkably easy to use and even Claris Works or PowerPoint are usable by older children.

(7–11)

6   **Short regular sessions are best for practising skills on the computer.** This is true for IT skills, as well as drill and practice programs in other areas like maths or spelling.

7   **Try the Internet.** Almost everything on the WWW seems to be copyright free, so use it for finding relevant pictures and information for pupils to include in desktop publishing, which is related to a topic or theme. Do check each site before you start downloading – just in case.

8   **Think of other aspects of ICT.** Try tape recording, faxing and video. Annoy some education ministers, and use calculators! They are all relatively accessible these days and can generate valuable discussion of IT experiences and applications.

9   **See that IT is mentioned in every other subject's planning.** Every subject coordinator should be looking for opportunities to use IT in their subject areas, and if they aren't, get them to (or at least raise the idea)!

10 **Make it fun!** Using the computer creatively in music and art can be motivating and rewarding for a range of pupils. Indeed, it can be the best way to cover certain aspects on the National Curriculum for IT, for instance, modelling can be a difficult strand to cover. Getting children to use a simple musical composition program can provide excellent opportunities for modelling. Just by changing an instrument in an existing composition to see what it sounds like is modelling! If you can get them to compose their own stuff and they adapt, speed up, slow down, changing instruments etc, then that is even better. Similarly, using different effects in a painting program on the same picture can be a great way to discuss pattern, texture, colour, line, tone, shape, form and space in art, and to use IT to explore these aspects into the bargain.

11

Planning for continuity in IT

This is really an issue for the whole school and you should not be tackling it on your own. Most schools will have procedures for handing on records, but you may still need to make sure you are not just repeating skills and using programs the pupils have used before. The following suggestions may help you to get started on this.

1 **Know what is expected of you.** This should be in the school policy and scheme of work, but if you aren't quite sure, check with a senior manager or the IT coordinator before planning your own work in any depth.

2 **Find out what pupils have already done.** There should be some records from last year, either directly indicating what pupils have done in IT, or indirectly if there are copies of word processing or pictures in children's records.

3 **Know how the previous teacher organized access to the computer.** You may want to alter how you manage it, but at least you might start with a system that is familiar to the pupils.

4 **Find out what your pupils do at home.** Some pupils will have wider experience of ICT at home. It can be useful to train these pupils as experts or helpers to get peer support established. Be careful, however, to avoid pupils without ICT opportunities at home from feeling disadvantaged.

5 **Get your own routines established.** For instance, if you want your pupils to get the next pupil when they have finished with a machine, and to record what they have done, get a system going early on in the year. Like everything, it is hard going to start with but pays dividends in the long run.

6 **Have a clear idea of where you are trying to get to.** If you know what sort of things you want them to be able to do in word processing or painting using a toolbox program, you stand more chance of developing the relevant skills to the right level.

7   **Use a tick list to keep track.** Simple, easy to interpret records of what pupils have done is the first step. They will help you keep track of what the children have done and help to ensure equality of access. Such records will provide useful evidence for the next teacher, and will be valuable when inspections are due. Reviewing the list can then lead on to effective assessment. (See Chapter 6.)

8   **Concentrate on transferable skills.** Learning the intricacies of a complex program that the children will never see again is inefficient. Identifying skills in word processing, such as 'cut and paste', is more likely to ensure a progression in skills. You wouldn't expect all children to pick up new mathematical skills the first time. You would usually cover a basic concept several times, perhaps in different ways, before moving on. Good practice in ICT is just the same.

9   **Agree which programs different year groups will use.** There is no point in each year group using different word processors for example. There should be overlap from year to year, maybe even throughout a Key Stage so that skills and familiarity can be built upon and extended.

10 **Be creative, too!** Can you think of a *different* activity for developing word-processing skills this year? Just because you have done it one way before doesn't mean it is the only way. As long as you cover the necessary skills or learning outcomes, a new approach is worth a try. It also stops *you* from becoming set in your ways, and allows you to discover new and better tricks.

Chapter 3 IT as a Cross-curricular Subject

IT can find its inspiration and context within the rest of the curriculum. It can support, enhance and extend learning in many other subject areas. It can also be an excellent source of inspiration and motivation, but often ICT computers are used primarily as a source of 'Drill and Practice' (sometimes referred to as 'Drill and Kill') activities. This situation can cause stagnation and does not promote IT or ICT skills in any useful way.

In this chapter, we focus on how ICT can be used primarily to support other areas of the curriculum, but with the caveat that all such work can be valuable to both. While we would not like to suggest that you should be putting everything discussed here into practice immediately; being aware of the potential and the possibilities may help you both to plan and to implement the use of ICT more effectively into your classrooms and into your teaching style.

12

Organizing IT work in other curriculum areas

The following four sections discuss in some detail the variety of ways in which ICT can be used and developed throughout the curriculum. However, many of the ideas discussed in the following chapters should probably be viewed in light of the possibilities there may be for how you can organize access to ICT equipment and resources. This can vary widely from school to school and from one education authority to another, but consider the possibilities before you write off an activity as being totally impracticable. The famous phrase from Health and Safety legislation, 'so far as is reasonably practicable', can be applied to organizing IT.

1   **Be prepared to be flexible.** It you genuinely want to get the best out of the opportunities presented by ICT, you have to be prepared to consider changes, even quite radical changes, to the way you work and the way you organize your classroom and resources.

2   **Try to consider possibilities, rather than put up road blocks.** Everyone has, at one time or another, opted out of doing something because it seemed impracticable. Before you do, try to consider what the best possible scenario for a task or experience might be. Then consider how close you could get to that with the resources available in your school. Consider whether other schools in your area, especially your feeder and transfer schools, may be able to help. Consider whether other local institutions, such as colleges, universities or libraries may be able to help. If it is a worthwhile experience, the extra effort may be time well spent. Of course, you will need to ask your headteacher, but you can still start the ball rolling.

3   **Be prepared for a bit of upheaval.** Because ICT can be used throughout the curriculum, it may be appropriate to move resources around, especially if you have a classroom organized into learning areas. There is little point

in having a computer sat in the language area while it is being used in a science investigation. Here, it needs to be seen as a piece of scientific equipment. So, if possible, try to use it as such.

4   **Consider the needs of the activity.** For some tasks, managing with one computer and spreading the work over a fair time is not only reasonable, it can be the most effective method. But for other tasks a greater level of access may be essential. Consider the options. Just borrowing two or three extra machines from other classes for a morning could considerably enhance an activity. Ideally, your school might set up a dedicated resource room, but where this is not practical, possible or not available, try other methods. Furthermore, a dedicated resource room has its own drawbacks, not least the risk of sidelining computer equipment rather than main-streaming it.

5   **Consider whether the children need to have access to resources to learn.** There is no reason why children need to have access to ICT resources to benefit from them. You could use a floor robot to demonstrate an idea, and the children could then work on a task using pencil and paper. They could compare solutions and try out ideas by pretending to be robots. Of course, it would be a shame if they never had the opportunity to try their ideas out for real, but the other options may make group work far more effective.

6   **Why not use technology as a teaching aid?** There is no reason to assume that children need to be sitting at the computer to make use of it. As long as the class or group are working where they can see it, you could use the computer to demonstrate ideas, a bit like a blackboard. You may have gathered some data in science work. You may want to discuss which would be the best sort of chart to use to present your information. If the data is put into a spreadsheet, you can produce several possibilities and discuss their merits before the children go off and produce their own charts with pencil and paper.

7   **Try to get others involved.** More often than not, it isn't practical or desirable for you to be directing and supporting the IT work in your classroom. There may be students, auxiliaries, parents or governors who would be willing to help out. An extra pair of hands can take away the need for reorganization, as the extra support will help to keep the children focused and on task.

8   **Consider whether you can use other spaces within school.** When working with floor robots, it may be appropriate to use the playground or corridors adjoining your classroom. When using sensors, control boxes and so on, having a computer on a trolley so that it can be moved around easily can be a real help.

9   **Get hold of a set of headphones.** There is no doubt that computers can interfere with the general peace and harmony of the classroom, and vice versa, especially with software that insists on playing mind-numbingly repetitive tunes all day. Many computers can have headphones fitted, and with an adaptor can take more than one set, turning your computer area into a quiet area and avoiding some of the distractions a computer can cause. This won't always be appropriate, but when practicable it can make life much more pleasant.

10 **Finally, ask for it!** In our experience, IT coordinators can feel very isolated when it comes to steering their curriculum area. Many would be only too delighted to have someone else making a few suggestions. If you feel you are missing an opportunity, why not ask to have a look through the huge pile of free catalogues your coordinator is bound to have stashed away. (It might be wise, however, to check that you aren't about to try to spend a budget that has already been spoken for.)

13

ICT in language

ICT can be used to support the development of language skills throughout a child's schooling. It can also be used to provide contexts and opportunities for the use of language that would be hard to achieve otherwise. This can include everything from a precise and concise message for use in e-mail to reading and making sense of information from teletext, or from a recording of a radio news bulletin to developing pencil control using a special 'mouse pen' on the computer. What follows are some ideas that might help you make the most of these opportunities.

1   **Find out what sort of additional hardware you have available.** Your IT coordinator should be able to tell you whether you have additional hardware, such as concept keyboards, touch screens or 'mouse pens', (great for practising pencil or brush control with basic software such as paint programs). Also, tape recorders, videos, TVs with teletext, CD-ROMs, Internet access and the like can all provide good opportunities for language work.

2   **Find out what sort of additional software you have available.** There is certainly plenty! Talking books are widely acknowledged as being excellent for developing early reading skills, with the additional bonus that they are basically self-supporting once the pupils have the idea of the intuitive controls. You will need software to drive concept keyboards. You can get programs that are designed to help with letter formation – copy and match programs often have activities that develop a range of early literacy skills. There are a huge range of multimedia CD-ROMs that are fairly self-supporting once the basics have been mastered. Your IT coordinator should be able to provide you with further information on software that will support your language teaching.

3   **Try to identify a couple of programs that best suit your needs.** It is unrealistic, and possibly counterproductive, to try to use too many different programs. To get the best from them, you need to put in time and effort (not necessarily your own time and effort!). Give your class

time to get to grips with programs, making sure everyone gets a go. Then try to make it available so that the pupils get the chance to extend and consolidate what they have learnt. They can't do this if there are too many programs to choose from.

4   **Try to get the best out of what you have got.** Concept keyboards, for instance, are incredibly versatile. They can be used for very early literacy skills in nursery and reception, where simple sentences can be built up using sight vocabulary and picture clues. They can provide sources of information in, say, history work, where pressing a picture of an artefact presents information about that artefact on the screen. They can be a way of communicating information, where the children design overlays and program the computer to present their ideas to others.

5   **Use word processors to their full potential.** Obviously word processors are useful for presenting written work neatly but, if used well, can do a lot more besides. Pages can be set up that act as a stimulus for written work. A piece of clip art or decorative border that may help inspire creative writing can be prepared in advance. They are perfect for drafting, editing and redrafting work because making alterations is so easy. They often contain spell checkers and the clarity of the text can make identifying errors much easier. They are too expensive to be used just as typewriters, so try to use their full potential!

6   **Use technology for sources of inspiration for language work.** Taped interviews with important people, news reports, teletext and so on can be great sources of inspiration for research and creative writing activities with older and more able pupils.

7   **Use technology to record ideas for written work.** Clearly, word processors are great for recording ideas once keyboard skills have been acquired and access is available, but other forms of technology can be useful for assisting with language work. Get those children who find it difficult to maintain direction in their work, perhaps due to slow or illegible handwriting, to record stories or ideas onto audio tape. By listening to what they recorded, they can then copy out a piece at a time, helping to keep them focused on the task.

8   **Use technology for recording ideas for speaking and listening.** Consider tasks such as preparing a news bulletin or play pupils have written for recording on video or audio tape, or enhancing role play activities with an old telephone or old radio, or retelling familiar stories for others to listen to. Technology provides some of the best opportunities and motivation to talk *and* to listen.

9   **Try not to be afraid of apparently complex computer activities.** If the thought of letting your class have a go at multimedia authoring rather chills your blood, don't let it. It is amazing how much children can achieve with even just a little nudge in the right direction. If you learn the very basics to get them started, they will probably discover a surprising amount for themselves, then they will teach you (could this be pupil-lead INSET?).

10   **If you have access to the Internet, use it.** For developing higher order reading skills, such as reference and research work, what could be better than access to the largest, continuously growing body of information ever collected? There are security issues, but software that provides some protection is freely available. You could even download whole sites for use off-line; this way you get to vet the sites' content.

14

ICT in maths

ICT can offer a range of contexts and opportunities for developing and extending mathematical work at any stage of educational development. Often without even realizing it, children can be acquiring and consolidating mathematical skills as they work. So look out for the possibilities. Here are some to start with.

1   **Find out what sorts of additional hardware you have available.** Ask your IT coordinator about floor robots, remote-controlled toys and resources that will help you use them effectively. You will need to see your maths coordinator about calculators and support materials for using them.

2   **Find out what sorts of additional software you have available.** As with packages for language work, there are many pieces of software that can be used as drill and practice for basic number skills. Everything from early number recognition to number bonds to times tables to simulated adventures involving mathematical problem solving can be useful. Your long-suffering IT coordinator should be able to make a few appropriate suggestions!

3   **Remember that floor robots can be used even with very young children.**
(3–5) The controls on many of the more popular floor robots are very clear and they often use non-standard units of measurement, allowing for comparative measurement, estimation, investigation and discussion with small groups of early years children.

4   **Remember that floor robots can be used even with older children.** The
(7–11) beauty of controlling floor robots is that the work children do is as hard as the problems they are set. These robots can often be used with standard units of measure and degrees of turn. They can hold complex sequences of instructions to solve problems that may require investigation, measurement, calculation, recording, team work and experimentation to get right.

5   **Try to get one generic maths program that may be used throughout the year.** You will probably need a package that allows you to work on data handling and perhaps spreadsheet work, and a LOGO package can be very useful. As with all generic programs, try to get one that suits your age group and stick to it, as the children's familiarity with the program develops, so does their ability to use it independently. If possible, try to get one that is used throughout your key stage to promote this aim.

6   **Keep the number of drill and practice programs to a minimum.** To get the best out of a program it is usually better to keep it around for a while. If you organize it so that each child has a go and then never sees it again, you are missing out on one of the best motivational factors – trying to get a higher score than last time! Watch children (and adults!) using computer games to remind yourself how addictive this factor can be.

7   **Try to get hold of drill and practice programs that are flexible.** See your IT coordinator about drill and practice or simulated adventure software that the children will not have seen in previous year groups. Most programs will have some degree of control over the complexity of the problems built in, often found under the 'teacher controls' menu. Try to set it so that the program challenges the children, but not so high that they rely heavily on your assistance.

8   **Consider how you are going to ensure that everyone has the same opportunities.** If you are not going to have the use of these sorts of programs as planned activities recorded by you, the chances are that some children will dominate the use of them. You could try getting them to record when they have used the program, even to record how far they got. At least you will know who to encourage and who to point in different directions!

9   **Look out for effective support packs.** Many simulated adventures come with resource or activity packs, ie, collections of worksheets that go along with a piece of software. Sometimes they provide good support materials, with work that you can do away from the computer, but often they are to be used alongside the computer. If you only have one machine in your classroom, using these materials can become a logistical nightmare.

10   **Do not underestimate the power of peer tutoring.** Children working in pairs on mathematical tasks teach each other very effectively. Just try sitting and listening to the quality of the discussions and cooperation going on between two children trying to solve a mathematical problem using a floor robot if you want proof! Often, when using ICT-based resources, less (of you) is more! Sometimes, very little teacher input is required. Also the 'expert/apprentice' model of working for disseminating knowledge, understanding and strategies, can work very well in these contexts.

15

ICT in science

ICT fits into the science curriculum in a variety of ways. It can be used as an experimental tool, for gathering and exploring data, for recording information and presenting ideas, and even for consolidating basic concepts. What you can achieve is limited largely by what you have access to but, with even quite limited resources, you can provide effective support for your science work using IT.

1   **Find out what sort of additional hardware you have available.** Another visit to your IT coordinator should give you an idea of the sorts of hardware you have available. Ask about sensors or data logging equipment for measuring work. Ask about control boxes that can be used to explore electrical circuits and conductors, as well as actually controlling powered apparatus.

2   **Find out what sort of additional software you have available.** While you are there, ask about simple spreadsheets and database software. Ask about any simulated adventures that might cover relevant scientific concepts and about the software that you should use alongside the available hardware. Ask about CD-ROMs if appropriate, many are geared specifically to scientific concepts.

3   **Don't expect to be able to do it all at once.** If your school is well resourced, the possibilities and the opportunities you will be able to offer may be very different. It takes a lot of time and effort both to get to grips with new resources and to integrate them into your teaching. Over time you will be able to incorporate more into your work, but don't try to do it all at once.

4   **Try to take it one step at a time.** If you want to get the children in your class to use spreadsheets to record results of tests, they will need to do a bit of work first. Playing simple number function games in maths, taking some prepared data and drawing different charts and graphs, even just using it as if it were a glorified calculator will help them to become familiar

with what a spreadsheet can do. This understanding is very important if they are to get any benefit from using spreadsheets in scientific investigations.

5   **Remember that databases can be an excellent place to start investigating.** There are many aspects of science work that do not lend themselves to practical investigations, but databases on CD-ROM can still offer potential for exploration. For instance, if you were to discuss the differences between amphibians and reptiles, searching a database and noting characteristics of each could provide a stimulus for a great deal of debate and further investigation.

6   **Remember that computers are great for sorting and classifying.** Even in the early years, computers can be used for basic scientific work. If a child can 'point and click', they can pick up and sort information on a computer screen. Try the various 'My Worlds' screens for instance, or a picture-based concept keyboard overlay for recording what they did.

7   **Try using data logging equipment in group work.** Giving every child the opportunity to set up and carry out an experiment using sensors and so on would probably take a very long time! However, setting up an experiment with a group of 10 or so is far more realistic. As long as each can see the computer screen, then each can participate equally in the investigation.

8   **Try using technology to take the drudgery out of recording.** Children sometimes find it tough to investigate and to record at the same time. The use of the school's video camera or an audio tape machine may provide a more reliable system for recording. It may also provide one of the best sources of motivation and discussion you could hope for. Photographs are a lot more accessible and easier to manage, and they can also be extremely effective.

9   **Try using technology to take the drudgery out of reporting.** Children can often find reporting scientific investigations a long and boring process. Could they present their ideas on video? Could they make a picture of the investigation using a digital camera, and then talk about it? Perhaps a computer-generated chart as the centre-piece for a presentation to the rest of the class would provide more interest.

10 **Remember that modelling can be a valuable, but complex process.** In theory, computers are perfect for modelling events and trying out possibilities. In practice this is true, but they neglect to tell you that setting up reasonable models, and making it clear what these models are supposed to represent, can be really tough. You will find that it is much easier to stick to published software, unless you are a bit of a whiz!

16

ICT in foundation subjects

While the current trend is away from foundation subjects and towards the 'basics', there is still a clear need, and legal requirement, to develop children's understanding of life beyond English, maths and science. Once again, technology has a valid role to play, particularly in those areas of the curriculum where 'hands-on' experience is not easy. Here are some ideas to get you thinking of better ones!

1 **You need to be aware of what is available.** Perhaps by this time, if not done already, your IT coordinator will have decided to put together a list of what is available. Better still, such information will be included on core planning sheets, where resources may be listed and possibilities briefly described.

2 **Research sources of information and data.** Prepared data, such as well presented information on CDs and so on, can give a really good focus to study in geography, history, art, music and even technology as well.

3 **Identify simple sources of information.** The talking story book idea has been extended and adapted and now there are talking non-fiction books, too. With a little support and some purposeful structure to their work, even quite young children can start to carry out research work.

4 **Find resources that enable comparisons.** Many educational software developers have been putting together collections of photographic evidence, and occasionally video footage, together with a few notes and a searchable index to allow children to draw comparisons between, say, physical features of the local landscape and other, more varied land forms, or their own and others customs and practices.

5 **Get a couple of historical simulations.** There are quite a few of these around. They get the children involved in the subject they are studying at a more personal level, where the children are making discoveries and establishing links for themselves.

6   **Look out for simple-to-use databases.** If you want to get children into research and reference work, try making a class database – a place to collect the information you have gathered about a topic from various sources. This can provide a good purpose to a task and will teach them a great deal about how information can be stored, sorted and classified.

7   **Get a good, easy-to-use paint program.** A good paint package can be worth its storage space in gold. While it can allow children to put together illustrations for desktop publishing activities and so on, it can also be used to work in a way that can be too frustrating when done in a traditional approach. While many simple paint packages are a bit crude, they do allow children to experiment. This allows you to claim with justice that you are using computers to model situations. Illustrating work in different curriculum areas with the same program will develop key ICT skills and support different subjects.

8   **Consider simple drawing and design programs.** These are especially useful in technology, where a design can be repeated and altered fairly subtly several times without the need for starting again. There are a few programs designed specifically for this purpose that are extremely easy to use. With some, you can even test out your design on the computer to see if it works!

9   **Find suitable sites on the web.** If you have access to it, it is amazing how many libraries and museums have web sites. Just looking at one with a small group of children could open up many new avenues of study. Not only will it give access to new and previously unobtainable sources of information, but it will give children new ideas about how they might organize and present their own work in future.

10   **Make collections of clip art.** While it might seem like a bit of a cop-out, clip art provides instantly effective results which children love. They can provide a stimulus for written work, for example, pupils can write explanations of what a Victorian lady is wearing or how a steam engine worked, and so on.

11   **Look out for freebies.** Many more institutions and companies are putting together CD-ROMs that promote their interests, but that educate, too. Obviously, the World Wide Web is a good source of freebies as well. You may not like the idea of using the Internet in class, but there is no reason why it shouldn't provide you with the information you need to help you to teach!

12   **Use desktop publishing.** Possibilities include creating a history time line, or an annotated map for geography, a design for technology or a portfolio of pictures in art.

Chapter 4 Supporting Special Educational Needs with IT

ICT is an excellent tool to support children with Special Educational Needs. It can give them access to an appropriate curriculum. However, the wide range of special needs to be catered for, and the range of contexts in which such work might be undertaken, means that this is not a straightforward process. Individual children will need individual educational programmes, different support systems and activities, access to different hardware and software, and all of this needs to be managed by the individual class teacher, perhaps in consultation with senior management, and people in roles such as the Special Educational Needs Coordinator (SENCO) and the IT coordinator.

A lack of knowledge about what is achievable in such cases is perhaps the greatest obstacle to getting the very best out of what is available. In this chapter we discuss what is possible and how to exploit its potential. Computers have the potential to extend the learning of *all* pupils and that is precisely the challenge.

We would like to stress that our tips in this chapter are general suggestions, intended to help the non-specialist class teacher or SENCO. For a wide range of further suggestions on helping pupils with special educational needs, not restricted to their usage of computers, we suggest that you have a look at another whole book in this series, *500 Tips for People working with Special Needs* by Betty Vahid, Sally Harwood and Sally Brown.

17   Deciding on appropriate input devices
18   Adapting computer interfaces
19   Developing activities
20   Developing support for children with SEN
21   Stretching more able children

17

Deciding on appropriate input devices

Although there are a great many additional pieces of hardware you can strap on or plug into your ICT equipment to make it more appropriate for children with specific needs, there are also a few things to consider about the sort of hardware you should get in the first place. We share below a few ideas to take into consideration.

1   **Try alternatives to mice.** If children find it difficult to use a mouse because of coordination problems or because they simply can't hold a mouse, there are several other devices that might help. Some of these are described below.

2   **A track ball.** A very simple alternative that is basically an upside down mouse. Instead of moving the mouse so that the ball underneath rolls along the table top, you roll the ball with your fingers. Children using this sort of device will need reasonable hand–eye coordination, but it does make clicking the mouse button in the right place much easier. The larger the ball, the easier it is to control.

3   **Joystick**. This is a fairly straightforward alternative to the mouse and a device that still needs a reasonable degree of hand–eye coordination, but can be used with parts of the body other than hands. Many children (not to mention adults!) develop a good degree of control of joysticks by playing with computer-based games.

4   **A touch screen.** This is the most expensive of these devices but the easiest and most intuitive to use. There are various types, but basically they all work by putting a touch-sensitive, see-through screen in front of the computer monitor. Children can then select and move objects on the monitor just by touching the appropriate points on the screen.

5   **Concept keyboards**. Concept keyboards are great for all manner of ICT-based activity. They can be designed to handle everything from simple text input to reference and research work. Many can also be used to guide an on-screen pointer, although if a program to make this work is not included with the keyboard driver software, you may need to find someone who has had a lot of experience with programming concept keyboards.

6   **Headphones**. Almost all computers will have a jack socket for speakers. Speakers give general sound and may add significantly to background noise in the classroom. Working in these conditions is distracting and could be impossible for children with mild hearing difficulties. You can usually plug headphones into the speaker sockets, although do be aware that sometimes a comfortable volume setting for external speakers can be very loud when using headphones. A splitter plug to run two sets of headphones from one socket costs less than £2 from electrical chain stores.

7   **Alternative keyboards**. Some educational suppliers have been marketing adaptable and adapted keyboards. There are large, clear keyboards with keys shaped like lower case letters; ones that have letters set out in alphabetical order; ones that use picture inputs; ones that can be split and angled to meet the users' hands more easily. You will need to check that the keyboards you might want will work with your computers, but these sort of adaptations may well help to improve access for children with poor visual discrimination or coordination problems. Remember, however, that you may well want your special needs pupils to progress towards being able to work with the sorts of keyboard in everyday usage, and using an alphabetical one could mean they have to relearn the position of keys when moving to the endemic 'qwerty' keyboard.

8   **Identify key keys.** As a cheaper alternative to buying an adapted keyboard, suppliers also offer products that adapt keyboards cheaply and easily. Coloured stickers that you stick on to the keys of your keyboard (eg, delete, tab and return – if they are not already labelled) or guards that hide unnecessary keys can be useful.

9   **Switches and pads**. The most basic input devices are simple switches that allow for very basic control of the computer or other devices. They are appropriate for those with fairly severe physical difficulties, but are also great for use with control boxes and so on.

10 **Remember that if it's good practice for SEN, it's good practice**. The kinds of adaptations and supports that you may want to build in to support those with special needs will almost certainly provide useful support to those who don't have such needs. So spending money to support one child will probably be beneficial for a great many more – it may help to justify the investment!

18

Adapting computer interfaces

A great deal can be achieved in adapting your computer to fit the needs of pupils with special requirements. Often such changes can be achieved very simply, and sometimes simple and relatively cheap pieces of software can make a considerable difference. The following suggestions might trigger your imagination about where to start.

1   **Start somewhere easy.** Many computers and operating systems come with simple tools that allow you to adapt the way information is displayed on the screen. All modern computers have ways of adapting screen resolutions, background colours, menu and dialogue fonts, and so on.

2   **Consider whether changing the screen resolution might help.** This is just a way of determining how many parts of what is displayed on the screen is split into. The lower the resolution, the bigger the things on the screen appear to be. To help a child who is mildly visually impaired, or has trouble with visual discrimination, turn the screen resolution down (how this is done varies widely, if unsure, ask your IT coordinator or see the handbook).

3   **Find out if your computer has an adaptable interface.** For instance, an Apple Mac will have a thing called the Launcher. Launcher is just an alternative way for getting to files and programs. It is adaptable so you can restrict certain children's access to certain programs and files. It can even be adapted for individual pupils and it's free!

4   **Put folders and programs where pupils can get at them.** Most computers now have Graphical User Interfaces – basically the pictures that represent files and folders that you see on the screen. These interfaces are usually fairly adaptable. Try setting up short cuts (since Windows 95) or aliases (Apple Mac), so that the icon for a program, or a folder for work, is the first thing a child can see on the screen. This way they don't have to remember complex journeys through files and folders to find what they want. They are less likely to stray into areas you don't want them to find, too.

5   **Try changing background colours.** Modern computers can have the patterns and colours that cover the screen changed and adapted. Children who have problems with visual discrimination may find certain background colours much easier to work with.

6   **Adapt pointing devices.** Most modern computers have some kind of input device to control an on-screen pointer. Sometimes this pointer can be very difficult to see, but many of these on-screen pointers can be adapted to make them larger and clearer, or to make them appear in brighter colours, or to give them a three-dimensional appearance. Your IT coordinator or ICT centre should be able to help. If not, try ringing your local educational ICT supplier for software.

7   **Try third party solutions.** Some software developers have tried to tackle the problem of boring interfaces, that were after all, designed for adults to use. There are a few programs that will adapt the desktop of your computer and make it more child-friendly. One turns programs into items on a child's desk and files into books or folders on a shelf, almost as if everything were stored in a child's bedroom or study. Ring your supplier or ICT centre for advice.

8   **Look out for 'short cuts' palettes.** Most generic programs, word processors, databases, spreadsheets and art packages have buttons around the screen that help users to control what happens on the screen. Some also have the option to add more buttons by using a short cuts palette. Buttons, with helpful icons, such as print, save, new folder, speak, page setup, and so on can sit discretely in the top right-hand corner of the screen, so that children don't need to remember which menu to go to. Once more, see your coordinator or the manual!

9   **You may want to consider voice navigation.** This is where, in theory at least, a computer can respond to voice commands using a small microphone on a stand. As of 1998, this technology is still relatively new and some problems have been reported, but technology marches on so quickly that it would definitely be worth investigating as a way to support children who cannot control other input devices at all. Anticipate, however, that voice navigation may not have the desired effects if the machine is sited in a noisy classroom.

10   **On-screen concept keyboards might be worth a look.** Programs, such as Clicker (which can be used with Acorn, Mac and Windows), work just like a concept keyboard, but are actually displayed on the screen and work with almost any word processing package. These can be very motivating and a flexible source of support; children can simply take it or leave it!

11 **Look in catalogues and leaflets**. The range of devices and software for supporting access to IT for children with special needs grows and changes rapidly. It will always be worth checking through up-to-date catalogues to see if there are solutions that might help you with a specific educational special need in your classroom.

19

Developing activities

It often seems that, given the time and money, you could use ICT to totally transform the way you work with children with special needs. However, finding the time and money to develop all the activities you can think of is almost certainly impossible. A little planning and the repetition of some simple concepts may help you to decide where to start.

1   **Before starting to develop activities for specific individuals, look at their statements or Individual Education Programmes (IEP).** These documents will help you identify specific needs and, therefore, the sorts of activities that might be appropriate.

2   **First of all, consider what minor adjustments could be made to existing activities.** Obviously it is going to be easier and quicker to adapt activities that you are already using. Can you, for example, take a word processing activity set up for more able children, and put together a concept keyboard overlay that will support those with special needs? Also, bear in mind the other adaptations suggested in the previous section.

3   **Look at commercial solutions.** One of the major problems with supporting special needs with IT is that no two special needs are exactly alike. Sometimes commercially produced solutions to learning difficulties, such as dyslexia, can be a good starting point. Consider whether such software can be adapted to support individual circumstances, and ring suppliers to see if you can arrange a free trial of the software before you buy it.

4   **Go for adaptable software.** There is an increasing number of programs that act as a framework to support a wide variety of 'add-on' software. Programs such as 'My World' and 'My World II' for Acorn and PC, have a vast number of add-on activities that cater for a wide range of abilities, and that can be used in a wide variety of contexts. If you can't buy the activity you want, perhaps you can adapt others or just be very fussy as to which add-ons you use.

5   **Try to make the most of what you have got.** One thing that inhibits the efficient use of ICT equipment is a lack of knowledge about what is achievable. Knowing the extent to which some of the software and hardware you have in school can be stretched means that you can get the best out of it. Many manuals now contain an overview near the front. It may be worth having a look before you go out and try to get to grips with something entirely new and expensive!

6   **For tackling problems with literacy, try talking word processors.** Many schools will have access to a simple talking word processor. These programs can 'read' the children's work, either word by word or sentence by sentence. Studies have shown that talking word processors are not only motivating, but they help children correct work independently, help with phonemic awareness and can considerably enhance reading and spelling skills.

7   **You could try talking books, too.** There is a significant amount of research that suggests that talking books can have considerable impact on the performance of both beginning and struggling readers, especially in Key Stage 1 and early Key Stage 2. However, the activities can be a bit limited and short-lived. Try using the images from the books to make overlays for concept keyboards for story structure or sequencing activities. You could use pictures of characters as a stimulus for further work with talking word processors. You could focus on key words within the books, counting how many times they occur for example. The possibilities are extensive!

8   **Don't be frightened of what sounds very complex.** Multimedia authoring sounds difficult, this is primarily because the multimedia software we see is complex, but multimedia simply allows you to add a bit of sound to text and pictures. With a microphone and a simple multimedia authoring program, you can develop basic activities with vocal prompts at complex points or in response to their input – even voice prompts at the level of 'try again', and 'well done' can guide children through simple tasks on a computer and will help enhance independent work.

9   **See if software has built-in differentiation.** If you are using software to develop or consolidate knowledge in other curriculum areas, see if the level at which it operates can be altered to meet the requirements of lower-attaining pupils.

10 **Do not underestimate the 'motivation factor'.** It is often very surprising how much apparently less able pupils can do on computers. There are many ideas about why this is, including suggestions that pupils look more closely when they are motivated so mistakes are easier to see, and the fact that errors are easy to change means that mistakes are less frustrating. But, perhaps, it is simply that children find computers, and what they can achieve when using them, exciting and interesting so they try that bit harder. Nothing succeeds like success.

20

Developing support for children with SEN

Clearly, you are not going to be able to support children with special needs in the way you might want to every time you would like to. Sometimes, using computers can actually save you time in class, but often additional support *will* need to be provided. Managing and organizing such support to get the best from it is essential.

1   **Do your best to rope in other people.** These can include parents, governors, volunteers, grandparents and Uncle Tom Cobbley to help out in the classroom. It will also be worth asking an educational psychologist or the educational support services, who should be able to offer advice or even provide direct help in supporting children with special needs with ICT.

2   **Do your best to rope in people in the know.** People who have some familiarity with the children involved or the sorts of ICT work you want to undertake, or preferably both, will be able to support children with special needs on computer-based activities with relatively little input from you.

3   **Consider the use of peer tutoring.** Children often seem to be able to explain things to one another more effectively and succinctly than any teacher can. Someone who has just learnt something can remember *how* the light dawned, and this makes it easier to help someone else to learn it. They can often be relied upon to support their peers with a good deal of understanding and sensitivity, too.

4   **If the opportunity arises, try to train a parent or two.** If you work in a school that encourages parents to work in classrooms and to support all aspects of school life, see if you can track down a parent with some ICT experience early on. They could become an invaluable source of support for you and the children who most need it.

5   **Use printouts to help with the sequence of events.** In a specific activity there may be several steps. If you print out an example of each step along the way, you can then use them as teaching aids, and as *aides-mémoire*. This small additional support can guide those who have trouble remembering sequences of instructions, or who lack confidence, and allowing them to work through the task unsupported.

6   **Try making step-by-step cards.** As an adaptation of the idea above, writing or printing simple prompts on to a series of cards and fastening them together in the appropriate order might be all that is required to guide less able children through more complex tasks. If these can be picture clues, then the range of abilities you can support can grow even further. Look out for clip art collections aimed at education.

7   **Consider whether it is appropriate to get an auxiliary or support teacher trained.** Where specific needs have been identified and one-to-one support is recommended, see if you can either find the time (or ask your ICT coordinator) to train support staff in the use of appropriate software and hardware. You may be able to negotiate additional time for more worthy cases, such as during assemblies, break times of even lunch breaks.

8   **Ask about enlisting help from older children.** Recent reports suggest that mentoring – when an older child helps a younger child with a specific sort of task on a regular basis – is at least as beneficial for the helper as it is for the learner. Older children often accept responsibilities such as these extremely well and can be trained, to a certain extent, in what is and what is not appropriate when working with younger children who may be struggling a little.

9   **Never forget the value of experimentation.** Children with special needs know how to play with computers. It is perfectly possible that they learn just as much, if not more, when they are allowed to work with computers without any overt goal. Free experimentation can have a significant impact on the quality of more structured work later.

10 **Remember that ICT has a lot of pulling power.** If you are seeking additional support or funding to help support a child with special needs in school, and you can make a strong case that an increased ICT provision would help, you stand a good chance of attracting attention. Because ICT is the 'new' educational idea there is a good deal of desire to promote its use; you might as well try to get something for your trouble!

21

Stretching more able children

Many very able pupils find ICT a particularly motivating way to work. Don't forget that highly gifted children have their own kinds of special educational needs, and need to be kept interested and appropriately challenged. Besides, if they are not duly stretched, they can become disruptive or lose motivation. Giving them opportunities to work with technology, and ways to stretch their abilities and skills is a pathway worth taking.

1   **Use the never-ending activity.** Work with computers, floor robots, calculators and so on is perfect for more able children, mostly because the possibilities are endless and each new thing learnt opens up new possibilities, so keeping those children who always finish everything in half the time needed engaged in their work.

2   **Use ICT to provide contexts for open-ended investigation.** Some teachers find the idea of programming a computer daunting. But LOGO is a simple programming language, the basics of which can be learnt quickly, and which is well supported across the age range. Even better, some of the more creative LOGO programs or activities provide wonderful opportunities for open-ended investigation, problem solving, planning and communication, as well as developing useful mathematical skills. Even better, you don't need to know much to get them going, just the first few, obvious commands and some children will get the idea quickly.

3   **Set them a challenge.** If you have drill and practice software that is adaptable, crank the level up a bit and set your more able children a challenge. You could even run a handicap competition on the quiet!

4   **Remember, pupils can often teach themselves better than you can.** Given a purpose and a starting point, all children, but especially able children, test the boundaries of what is possible far more quickly than adults tend to do. Teachers should not be frightened of this, but should use it to their advantage. After all, there is no reason why they shouldn't teach you, is there?

5   **Keep the handbook handy.** When bright pupils get stuck using technology and want an answer that you don't have, give them the handbook. It is an excellent context for non-fiction reading and a good way of giving them control of how far they go! This tactic depends, of course, on your view of the truthfulness as well as usefulness of manuals.

6   **Try to keep reference and research material available, too.** If you can have a CD-ROM encyclopaedia handy, or perhaps a spreadsheet program for maths investigation, or even access to the Internet or a topic-related database, you will always have somewhere to go with children who learn quickly. All the better if you can have each of these at the same time. If you can direct able pupils to such resources, they will be positively engaged and you will be able to get on!

7   **Don't worry about blind alleys.** Just because they're clever doesn't mean they will get always it right. It is often tempting to guide children towards the 'correct' answer, but mistakes are valuable learning experiences and it doesn't hurt to get things wrong once in a while. This is especially true with ICT, because you have to learn how to get out of trouble, too! It can be damaging to protect pupils from ever making mistakes with technology.

8   **Let them teach.** As long as the children are fairly social creatures, quick learners can support others by acting as experts in peer tutoring situations. Clearly, you need to be careful, but evidence suggests that the expert will learn as well as the learner!

9   **Let them plan, or at least negotiate, what they might try.** Because they are bound to have their own ideas about what they want to do, you might like to encourage this. It is useful in such a situation to have a model or plan they can follow. Ideas for starting points can be found in books or from organizations like the National Association for Able Children. A good multimedia package like 'HyperStudio' (Roger Wagner, multi platform) has limitless possibilities.

10 **Try developing logic and critical thinking.** Some programs like 'The Logical Journey of the Zoombinis' (Brøderbund, Mac and PC) can be used by able five-year-olds, but will tax Oxbridge graduates! The only issue is: can you cope with your pupils solving logical problems that you can't?

Chapter 5   Resources for Teaching IT and ICT

Clearly, resourcing issues for ICT are relevant to the class teacher, but often remain the headache of the IT coordinator and senior management. But there are two sides to the problem of developing resources for the teaching of IT. This chapter is concerned with the sorts of resources that a teacher may use to support children during classroom work. We offer suggestions on resources such as work cards, effective starting points, targeting the use of the Internet, as well as how to get the best out of software such as talking books and CD-ROM materials.

22

What can what you've got do?

It is amazing what some computers and software programs can do. It is worth spending time learning about some aspects in detail. The following suggestions are things for you to do before getting your pupils to use computer-based resources.

1 **Use a computer yourself.** The very best way of finding out what a piece of software can do is by using it in real contexts. If you have a word processor that can create tables or a desktop publishing package in school, why not see if you can do *your* planning on it? Make sure you always word-process letters to parents, and so on. Ask whether end of year reports can be done on the computer. In the long run it *will* save you time!

2 **Sit and play.** The best bet is little and often (this applies to your learning as readily as to that of your pupils!). Learning all about all of the programs you have in a marathon session is impractical. You will learn more effectively if you can use the programs you have played with. If you want to use a new piece of software, don't play with it weeks in advance! Almost certainly, you will find that you will have forgotten much of what you learnt, within a week or so!

3 **Use what you have got.** ICT involves computers, calculators, program-mable robots and a whole host of other electronic devices. Some aspects of the National Curriculum require you to consider wider uses and ap-plications of ICT. Find out what you have actually got access to, and make your way through it a little at a time.

4 **Put yourself in your pupils' shoes.** Make sure you have worked through a program in the way you think your pupils might. It is amazing where clicking little fingers can end up! If you have been right through the activity that you want your pupils to do, you will have a real working knowledge and a fair idea of some of the problems that might crop up!

5   **Know your computer.** Different operating systems have different features and may let you do more than you think. For instance, most have ways of letting you take a snapshot of the screen for making instruction cards. Can you cut and paste between applications? Can you drag and drop files to the printer to make them print?

6   **Use a simple program to the full.** Learning how to use one program well is more important than knowing a little about a lot of programs. A simpler program is also easier to teach the pupils to use.

7   **Use only the bits of the program that are useful.** For instance, a painting package may let you do what you want, then you can copy or import what you need into a presentation or publishing program. There are a few different approaches to this, but most types of painting file can be used in desktop publishing packages, although may need a little trial and error to find the easiest way to do it.

8   **Identify what you want to achieve and then see if the program will do it**. It is easy to be seduced by fancy features; it is important to keep your eye on what it is you want the pupils to learn.

9   **Let the pupils find out more for you.** You will not have the time to exhaust all the possibilities in complex programs. A CD-ROM will have thousands of entries. Let the pupils play and explore, perhaps outside of lesson times, too, and then try to review their work with them, getting them to explain or show you bits that you didn't know about. Asking a couple of pupils to review a new CD-ROM over a few lunch times and then report to the class what they found out is good for them, and can be a practical way for you to become more familiar with the software, too!

10 **Plan to develop pupils' skills.** Perhaps set a task for them to learn how to use a new tool in a painting package or a new font in word processing, and then get them to write a report or make a few suggestions about how and when they might use what they have learnt in the future.

11 **Get the pupils to share ideas**. This could be in the introductory and plenary sections of lessons. Otherwise, encourage sharing during group work either at or away from the computer. You will probably find that they will tend to share ideas almost without you even noticing, but it is such a valuable opportunity that it should not be left to chance.

12 **Look for ideas on the WWW**. A list of suggested starting points is given in Appendix 3.

23

Starting points... for teachers

Often it is just a question of getting going. Once you have started, ideas will frequently lead to other ideas. The hard part is just getting started! It is worth having a look at the Internet resources, particularly the National Grid for Learning. Other possible starting points are given in Appendix 3 or are available on-line at http//www.staff.ncl.ac.uk/s.e.higgins/500tips

1   **You've made a start if you are reading this!** There are other books, newspapers and magazines that all have useful ideas you can use as a starting point, but the will to do it is nine-tenths of the battle.

2   **Start with something that catches your attention.** You are more likely to have success with something you feel enthusiastic about. This in turn may lead on to other ideas. Try a drawing or painting program to recreate painting styles of the old masters – spray-can tools are great for the impressionists! Or how about a book of your children's book reviews? Or a slide show of pupils' work to run on a loop for a parent's evening?

3   **Team up with a colleague.** Working with someone teaching the same age group and swapping resources is a good way to develop your ideas. If you are in a small school and are the only one teaching that age group, you may have a colleague in a neighbouring school you could collaborate with.

4   **Employ the best method for disseminating information – a cup of coffee!** Try discussing ideas, desires, aspirations and queries about what it is you think you should be able to do in the staff room. Your colleagues may not thank you for bringing up taboo subjects during break, but if you can get them to talk, you may well find there is a lot more understanding of ICT than you think. Also try more formal occasions, staff and key stage meetings, and planning sessions.

5   **Try the National Grid for Learning** (http//www.ngfl.gov.uk). It is designed to support practising teachers and has a wealth of information, ideas and resources for all areas of teaching, particularly literacy and numeracy. Most of (former) NCET or (present) BECTa's site is easy to access, too.

6   **Other web sites are also expanding rapidly, try visiting them.** It is worth developing your own favourite bookmarks of places to visit. A list of some possible starting points is given in Appendix 3, although don't forget that there will have been major changes in the time it took to get this book into print. Your LEA may well have an Intranet or web site that lists sites that they have helped to set up or support. These should provide links to sites whose content has already been checked, so are safe to use with children! Or try the *500 ICT Tips Site* for up-to-date links – see Appendix 3.

7   **The Internet has a vast source of free and shareware programs.** Some of them are not so good, many are valuable. They are usually organized by operating system (eg, PC, Mac, Acorn); then there will be different areas containing system, utilities and educational programs. A good place to start might be a web site by the mining company (http://www.miningco.com) or Tucows at (mic5.hensa.ac.uk/mirrors/tucows).

8   **Read magazines and software catalogues.** They will often give you a good overview of what is available and what you can do. The advantage of software suppliers' catalogues is that once you are on the mailing list you can sit back and wait for them to flood in (which they will do with startling regularity).

9   **Ask local resource centres.** They will sometimes have exhibitions and open days in addition to courses they are offering. These can be good opportunities to try out new stuff, and to talk to people who have much more time to find out about and to keep up to date with software and hardware developments.

10 **Visit other schools which may have exhibitions or displays.** These will give you ideas, even if the focus of the display is not ICT.

24

Starting points... for pupils

A range of ideas for getting going in the classroom can be helpful. The computer or other ICT resources can be used in a variety of ways, as either the main focus of a lesson, or as supplementary parts of computer activities, or as a resource simply available for pupils to use.

1   **Start activities away from the computer.** There are many occasions when the pupils do not need to begin an activity at the computer. If you are introducing the idea of a database, for instance, see if you can get hold of a real card index to show the concept behind a digital database.

2   **Try problem solving activities that can use the computer in a variety of ways.** The computer can be used as a log or diary by a group. A newsroom simulation uses the computer to deliver latest news to pupils at determined intervals. Computer sensors can help collect information when tackling a scientific problem, or a control box can give a high degree of control in a technology activity.

3   **Use task cards to get pupils to develop search skills.** Simply setting an open-ended task involving some form of investigation may lead children to use a CD-ROM encyclopaedia, the Internet, and so on. This way of working, where ICT is a part of a process rather than an end in itself, will lead to increased use of equipment as a tool to assist pupils in their learning.

4   **Use the computer as a resource for a group.** For instance, researching information for a writing task, a small group can share information they find in books, from CD-ROMs or from the Internet to help one another. You may have to limit how long each group gets to consult it. Deciding who in a group uses the computer will always be tough!

5   **Competition will motivate pupils**. Setting up a 'design an advert' competition for a local shop or company may also help community links, but it will certainly get the best out of the children. It will most likely get them to delve more deeply into the potential of the software you are using. If you agree to give only technical support (no assistance with the content at all), it will also provide good opportunities for problem solving and assessment.

6   **Try timed races to inject new fervour into familiar programs**. This need not just be in skill and practice programs. You could have a 10-minute writing or painting task to develop pupils' pace of work on the computer.

7   **Combine tasks.** A newspaper day (or maybe week?) or producing a brochure or class book can involve all pupils in using the computer, but at different times and in different ways. They can use it for research, art work, layout, and so on.

8   **Science or other curriculum areas may give you a starting point.** Here you may be able to use real data in an investigation or experiment. In art, try using a spray-can tool in a painting program to develop understanding of Monet's paintings, for instance.

9   **Pupils do not need to start activities from scratch.** Investigating a pre-prepared database is much more efficient when the focus is on asking questions and using evidence rather than collecting and entering the data. Finishing a story or picture, or editing a text with lots of examples of errors you want pupils to identify, may be a better way to use the computer to achieve your specific learning objectives.

10 **Show web sites of other pupils' work.** If you are going to get them to design and put together their own web site, or maybe present a project in hypertext, pupils will need to see examples of how it works. You can always download a few examples in advance of the lesson, so you can guarantee they will appear when you summon them.

11 **Publish information on the WWW or send an e-mail summary to another school.** You may agree to do a joint project with another school, say a local study. Your children can collect information and resources to prepare and send to the other school. This may give you a focus for a great deal of work away from the computer, which only uses the computer at the final stages of compilation or exchange.

25

Building in support for activities

Newer computers and software have a lot of built-in help features, and many older programs will have help sheets or cards written for them. It can be a real benefit to work out how to use these efficiently and effectively so that you can use your time with other pupils.

1 **Train the pupils to use the support.** Pupils will choose the easiest way to get help. Make sure that this is not you, or you will always be on call. Training pupils to use on-line help is hard. There can be a lot of reading involved and it can be quite hard to know where to start. You could pick out key features, copy and print them to make support materials that are easier to use.

2 **Use on-line help where it is available, and at a suitable level.** You will often get help or instructions as part of the program. Sometimes you can turn this feature on or off as required, only turn it off if you are supporting the children in a different way.

3 **Try 'tutorials' and 'wizards'.** They will often demonstrate how to use basic features of the program you want pupils to use. Sometimes they can be amazingly informative, but be warned, sometimes they can also be irritatingly unhelpful!

4 **Look for programs with good interactive help.** Not all programs have good help features; it is worth making sure new and complex programs have help features which pupils can use. If you want help features that are aimed at children, you need to go for educational software. Commercial software may have help built in, but it is usually at an inappropriate level for use in school.

5   **Help sheets and cards are worth your time and effort.** To begin with it is worth developing cards and notes for the most commonly used activities, such as saving and printing. Using screen shots and pictures is invaluable, and when you have made them, you may find staff use them just as much as the children. Try swapping these with other members of staff, and other schools. You can get more, and distribute yours even further afield by visiting edit at (http://www.editsite.demon.co.uk).

6   **Get the pupils to write a guide.** You can then get another group to test it out and improve it! This way you can really push the use of a piece of software forward and produce differentiated help sheets into the bargain.

7   **Use speech or sound features of a program.** Many word processors have speech built in, so having instructions which the computer can read out can offer support to pupils who need it. Sometimes you can record your voice and add instructions yourself.

8   **Use a cassette recorder to tape instructions on what to do**. As long as you have a couple of sets of headphones, step-by-step instructions can be followed, and at the same time, you are developing children's use of control by getting them to use the controls on a tape recorder to their full potential.

9   **Structure a series of tasks so that pupils' skills are developed**. Have a series of specific questions for pupils to find the answers to on a CD-ROM. Start with easy specific questions, then some that are more open. This is far better than a general instruction to 'see what you can find out about the Egyptians', for instance.

10   **Deliberately get things wrong when *you* try out a program**. It will help you design better instructions and support cards!

26

Targeting IT use

Schools can plan both how hardware and software are used over the course of the year as part of a program, but also how specific groups of pupils can be targeted to support their learning. The following suggestions may help you to fix your sights appropriately.

1   **Pupils do not all need to do the same thing.** As long as all pupils get a chance to develop their IT skills they do not all need to do the same activities on the computer.

2   **Identify specific opportunities for SEN pupils.** Practising particular skills frequently for short periods of time (15 minutes, three or four times a week) is likely to be beneficial (see Chapter 4). Don't just give them routine tasks, though!

3   **Identify specific opportunities for higher attaining pupils.** Investigating a database or spreadsheet with more complex questions might be a good starting point. Pupils need to be given different challenges to develop their thinking skills at an appropriate level rather that just kept busy with more of the same work on the computer.

4   **Train pupils to work to a deadline.** This will improve overall pace. Pupils *enjoy* using the computer, yet the reward they usually get for finishing a task is stopping work on the computer! You will need ways to keep up the pace of their work.

5   **Build in *lots and lots* of time for activities you want everyone to do.** A task that takes one pupil 30 minutes will take more than a fortnight if you only have one computer available!

6   **Be ruthless and give pupils who will get the most from an activity the most time.** You may want to make sure that over the term or the year this balances out. There is no point in giving them all equal access if they will not all *benefit* equally!

7   **Try to revisit skills over the course of the year.** It is probably better to ensure pupils have mastered a relatively small range of core skills in word processing, drawing or painting and data handling, rather than simply having had a go at a large number of programs.

8   **Timetable scarce resources.** If you have a small number of floor robots, or just one colour printer, decide how the equipment will best be used.

9   **Use scarce resources.** It follows on from the previous point that if it is your turn for the robot or colour printer, use it. Have something planned that you will do when your turn comes up, so you don't waste your valuable time thinking about what to do.

10   **If you can't use it, pass it on to someone else**. Where resources are limited you may decide you cannot use what you have got or, on some occasions when it is your turn, you may not be able to make the best use of it. Someone else may be waiting for the chance to try out an idea with the equipment.

11   **If an activity works, tell someone**. Sharing ideas with colleagues about what you have found to work well is the best way for you, in turn, to get information from them about what works well for them.

27

Maximizing potential

Schools cannot only plan how hardware and software are to be used over the course of the year as part of a programme, but also how specific groups of pupils can be targeted to support their learning. You will never have enough equipment to meet all your pupils' needs, so setting your priorities is essential.

1   **Pupils do not all need to do the same thing.** We've said this before, but we think it is worth repeating! As long as you have an idea of what skills the pupils are developing, they do not need to do identical tasks.

2   **Target groups of pupils to support specific skills.** You might have a group of pupils who could do with more work on punctuation. Set them a word processing task where they know that is the focus and it will help them. Another group might do a similar task but with an emphasis on using more descriptive words.

3   **Be clear about what you want pupils to learn.** If you aren't sure what it is you want the pupils to get out of an ICT activity, you won't know if it was successful. It is best when you can tell your pupils exactly what you are intending them to get out of an activity.

4   **Share the learning objectives with them.** Pupils will attend better to the relevant aspects of the task if you let them know why you want them to use the computer.

5   **Review the learning objectives with them.** If they know what they were supposed to be learning, whether it was spelling, or how to cut and paste, they should be able to tell you if they think it worked.

6   **Little and often is usually better than lots, but infrequently.** This is particularly true for developing skills. However that does not necessarily mean it needs to be drill and practice. Pupils could do a timed 'look over write check' spelling task on the computer which will also develop keyboard skills. They could also take a printout of what they had done for homework!

7   **Find more time for pupils to use the equipment.** With whole class introductions and plenaries in literacy and numeracy sessions, it is no longer possible to have the computers in use all of the time. Before school, break, lunch time or after school may all be possible if you can crack the problem of appropriate supervision and support.

8   **Get support.** Who can help you? The IT coordinator? A colleague, student, parent, or older pupil? When you want to get something new off the ground you may find an extra pair of hands helpful. With ICT you may expect it will be more difficult to get help. You may be surprised if you ask.

9   **Get things finished.** ICT tasks often take longer that planned. Anticipate this and have strategies to get things completed. You will feel better about ICT if you accomplish your goals.

10   **Look back!** Every now and then, think back to which ICT tasks and activities turned out to have high learning payoff for pupils, and which were interesting for you to set up and to support. Build on your successes. Also, look for which tasks did not work out in practice. Work out why. Was it the software, or was it the equipment, or was it the way the tasks were set up? How could you have another go with these tasks, this time making them work better?

Chapter 6   Assessing IT

Increasingly, assessment of children's abilities and progress is essential in every area of the curriculum to ensure that progress is consistent, planning is informed and teaching is as effective as it can be. Since IT is often taught as a cross-curricular subject, it can end up being left out of assessment procedures, and when it is included it is often in a very diluted form. If IT is to be taken seriously, it has to be assessed and, as IT becomes increasingly significant in political and educational thinking, it also becomes clear that the assessment of IT is not only sensible but inevitable.

In this chapter, we offer some tried and tested ideas for implementing effective assessment of IT, and on how assessment can be used to enhance teaching and learning.

28

Identifying opportunities for assessment

Assessment is often regarded as a complex area. However, you will automatically be assessing informally all the time you are teaching, and these informal assessments are very valuable in their own right. There are occasions when you will need to be more systematic in your judgements, and occasions when you need to record what you have assessed, too. The following suggestions may alert you to some things worth assessing.

1   **The most useful assessment is what you see pupils do, and what you hear them say.** Assessment is a continuous part of the teaching process, and you will see and hear a lot that gives you information about pupils' skills, knowledge and understanding when they are using ICT.

2   **Identify a specific focus in your short-term planning.** This might be an IT-related skill, or a skill in a different area which the pupils can demonstrate through their use of ICT. If you have done your short-term planning in some detail, you will also have recorded learning outcomes, and these learning outcomes can be assessed.

3   **Identify a learning outcome in terms of what the pupils will actually do.** This makes deciding on assessment criteria easier. When you identify what they will have to do, you will also have identified goals for that activity. If they attain these goals, then you know they possess the relevant skills and understanding or, indeed, that they are quick enough to have found an alternative strategy, which may be equally desirable.

4   **Identify different ways in which pupils can demonstrate their achievement of the learning outcomes.** It may be something they write, draw, say or even teach to another pupil.

5   **Cover different areas through your long-term planning.** Over the course of the year, your planning should indicate which key skills will be taught and assessed in IT. Therefore, over the year you will not only cover a broad range of skills, but you will also be able to assess these skills, building a fairly detailed picture of the links between IT and key skills.

6   **Ask pupils questions, and get pupils to ask each other questions.** These should focus on probing understanding, open-ended questions that start with 'why?', 'how?', 'what else?', and even 'so what?'

7   **Only record *some* of this.** You need to be systematic from time to time, but it may be best to let the whole picture to be built up in stages. You can't realistically assess everything in one go, so just record one step at a time.

8   **Assess *some* things from finished work.** There may be some things you can assess from the product of activities. You will need to know a lot about the conditions under which the activities were done, however. You might be able to work out pupils' skills at using different tools in a painting program from the finished picture. You will not be able to assess spelling skills if they have used a spell checker or dictionary, and so on.

9   **The software may have feedback for the teacher.** Some programs have a built in record keeping feature you can use. More complex (and expensive) packages like ILS (Integrated Learning Systems) have detailed reports for teachers.

10 **Involve the pupils.** Even in Reception and Nursery, children can make judgements about what they have learnt and how successful they have been. Their own understanding of what they can achieve will not only give you valuable information, it will also help them to develop new skills, or to develop further the ones they already have.

11 **Formal assessment needs definite goals.** If you are going to try to assess children's abilities in ICT formally, you need to know exactly what skills and responses you are looking for. If you are assessing IT through a specific task, look at which skills and understanding that task will require – those will be the aspects of children's learning that that task will be useful for assessing.

12 **Keep it simple, succinct.** This is sometimes called the KISS principle of assessment. An important aim of assessment is to help you as a teacher. If it doesn't, don't do it.

29

Practical assessment activities

Higgins' Educational Uncertainty Principle states that the more precisely you know about a pupil's performance (for instance where they are on a standardized test), the less useful this information is about their momentum of learning. You may get more helpful information for your teaching from observing them work, and in an open-ended task. This information is, however, less exact and comparable, and it takes longer to acquire. Generally speaking, in ICT you will find it more helpful if you assess them through the activities they complete than in setting up little tests. The following suggestions may give you some ideas for designing useful assessment activities.

1 **Ensure that pupils succeed.** You will get to know more about what they can do if they are successful. This may well mean offering support to push them on further, but it may just be a question of giving more time, allowing them to set their own challenges, and so on. Children tend to be overambitious rather than underambitious in ICT, so this isn't really all that much of a gamble.

2 **Make sure they show what they can do.** You need to decide if your task or activity really allowed them to demonstrate their skills. If it didn't, what did they demonstrate? Sometimes, you may need to be flexible and assess what they demonstrate, rather than what you hoped they might demonstrate!

3 **Listen to what they say.** Informal talk in an activity can reveal what children do (and do not) know. It can also demonstrate the extent to which their understanding of ICT stretches further than their actual skills (or, more rarely, vice versa).

4 **Use a familiar format.** Children can be thrown by a new program or situation and this may well restrict their performance. Therefore, as a general principle, don't use work on a new piece of software as the basis for formal assessment, or as a demonstration of understanding, although it may indicate which ICT skills are lacking.

5 **Plan an activity so that pupils can demonstrate a range of performance.** This is more efficient than single skill assessments. It may be sensible to try more open-ended activities so that performance can be judged by outcome, for example, how far the children managed to take the idea. Try assessing the writing of a story from start to finish. Can they load the program, enter and edit text, save, print...?

6 **Assessing understanding is challenging.** Assessing skills and knowledge is easier. You may get an impression of what they do understand if you get them to explain how they completed a task. This may well indicate both skills and knowledge.

7 **Share your judgements with other teachers.** This will help both you and your colleagues to agree in your judgements. In IT, coordinators might be good colleagues to start with, as it will let them know what you have been doing, too!

8 **Don't waste the results of effective assessments.** When they work well, use formal assessments as a summative record of pupils' achievement. It could well be the case that a report of the results of formal assessments says everything you could want a report on a child's abilities to say.

9 **Think twice before telling pupils the marks or levels.** Telling them their marks can make pupils focus on the end result of the test and not on their own effort, or the parts of the assessment they could improve. However, some could be spurred on by the incentive to improve on a mark. Use your judgement to decide which is the best option.

10 **Remember effective assessment should help you!** If you are fairly sure that it doesn't, either don't do it, or adapt it so that it is more useful to you or, failing all else, make sure that it takes up as little of your precious time as possible!

30

Using assessment to inform planning

Assessment is a vital part of the teaching and learning cycle. However, it assumes you can then alter or refine what you do next. If you have a fixed programme that will not alter after doing an assessment, why *are* you assessing? Consider the following before embarking on a new assessment plan.

1   **The time you spend on assessment should be proportional to the benefit *you* get from it.** If you, and the rest of the staff, are convinced that you can make gains in attainment through all-singing, all-dancing assessment procedures, go for it. If not, don't. Measuring a child every day will not make them grow any faster.

2   **Assess at the beginning.** Do this when starting a new theme, topic or unit of work to find out what pupils already know or can do. This could be through a class discussion, review of formal assessments, looking back at last year's scheme, or simply your reflections of what they achieved last time. If it is formally recorded, it can be an excellent source of evidence that will help refine your planning.

3   **Assess at the end to record what pupils have achieved.** This will help your evaluation of what you have done, so you can improve your teaching of that task next time, or adapt the task to meet pupils' identified needs more successfully.

4   **Don't invent new formats for recording assessment.** Someone, somewhere has done it before. And even if they haven't done it exactly the way you might want it, it is a lot easier (and quicker) to adapt someone else's ideas than to start from scratch.

5 **Use a computer to make lists and checklists.** It is efficient to prepare blank checklists by using a computer. However, it is then probably easier to photocopy a batch and handwrite the details of what is being assessed. Keep these checklists handy when you plan, to help to keep you focused on what the next step or two should be!

6 **Don't overestimate the value of formal assessment for planning.** It will usually confirm what you already feel you know and can, therefore, be very reassuring. It *is* worth paying attention to the surprises, too; they may point to something you have missed (they may also indicate poor assessment materials, or unwise choices of method, who knows?).

7 **Keep your planning flexible.** You may need to alter what you intend to do in the light of your assessment. If you tend to use fairly general statements in your mid- and long-term planning, then flexibility is assured. Include definite detail in short-term planning which can reflect results of recent formal or informal assessment.

8 **Don't be afraid to repeat assessments.** Children do not always learn in a neat progression. Often it takes a while for activities to sink in. More often than not, you can find different activities that use the same skills, so the children won't get bored.

9 **Keep skills planning separate from thematic work.** The theme or project or software you happen to have should not dictate what key skills you cover. You should decide on the key skills first, then map these on to the theme or project, and then to the particular software you use.

10 **Tell pupils how (well) they have done.** Rather than just give them marks, tell them *what* they did well, and *why* they did well. The more they know about your hopes and expectations, the easier it is for them to understand what they need to aim for themselves. Some may argue that this will ultimately stifle their creativity and individuality. If this is a concern, make sure that your expectations are that they will be able to set themselves challenges, ask themselves questions, and even decide upon whether they have achieved their goals or not!

31

Using assessment to develop teaching strategies

It can take a long time to use assessment to develop teaching. Even in the short term, however, data from assessments can help you to reflect on the effectiveness of an approach to a particular topic, theme or skill, and can help you focus on what works well. The following suggestions may help you to add more sense of purpose to your assessments.

1   **Look back at your 'before' and 'after' assessments.** Did the class make the sort of improvements you expected? Are there certain parts of the development they have demonstrated that are better than expected? Can you identify what it was that you said, or that they discovered, that might have brought about these improvements? If you can, you know what to stick with, and what you need to develop further.

2   **Ask pupils lots of questions.** You will get a good idea from their answers what the children really know and understand. Knowing this will help you decide where to go next. It may help you to identify opportunities for peer tutoring, self-help groups, and so on.

3   **Ask 'why?' questions.** This probes pupils understanding more, and at the same time makes them more aware of what they understand. The more aware they are of what they know, the better equipped they are to help one another. Here, being able to talk about it, and reflect upon it is a good step towards more independent learning.

4   **Get them to show you.** A demonstration of how to save or print a file on the computer either to you or to other pupils is a good way to assess how well they have been taught, and worthwhile consolidation for them, too.

5 **Eavesdrop and don't interrupt when pupils are collaborating.** When you barge into a collaborative conversation, pupils will assume you know what they have been talking about all the time. Listen first! This is easier when pupils are sitting at the computer and you can creep up behind them.

6 **Identify pupils who can, and get them to support those who can't.** Peer tutoring in pairs is one of the most effective means of support you can establish. In general, it is best not to have too great a difference of ability between the pair. A 'most able' pupil could help a 'middle range' pupil as a pair, and 'middle ranger' can help a lower attainer. However, don't underestimate the effects of friendship pairs.

7 **Identify common errors, and talk about these to a large group of the class.** There are many common misunderstandings and errors in using the computer, in areas such as understanding word-wrap (how the computer moves the text down to the next line), or clicking several times rather than waiting patiently, or assuming that you click OK or YES to every dialogue box!

8 **Assessing group work with one computer is appropriate.** Planning a group task where the computer is a resource or a tool is an efficient way to use it. It is harder to assess the results of group tasks, but pupils can learn a lot from each other.

9 **Assess individual work, too.** There are times when assessment of individual use of the computer may be needed. This can alert you to individual's particular needs. For example, some pupils never seem to have an opportunity to hold the mouse and may need their confidence boosting so they can develop their fine motor skills.

10 **Use your assessment findings to help children reflect on what they have done.** If you can find time to sit down with a child, or small group, and talk about what they have done and what that tells you about their abilities and development, it can have a significant impact on children's motivation and progress.

32

The use of self-assessment – a 10-step process

Involving pupils in self-assessment is teaching them to be responsible for their own learning, in essence to become their own teacher. The following steps provide a way to get started on this process.

1   **Identify small steps.** Break down an ICT task that you have planned into a series of relatively easily attained targets that the children will need to achieve.

2   **Make these 'can do' statements.** Write out each step or statement in child-friendly language so that the children will be able to use them, eg, 'I can print my work'.

3   **Involve the pupils.** Tell the children what they are going to be doing, and introduce them to the steps they may need to take. You can build in differentiation by getting the pupils to decide what they need to learn. This can be done on a one-to-one basis, as a small group or even as a whole class. As long as each child can decide upon a realistic starting point for themselves, there are gains to be made by using self-assessment.

4   **Make sure they can do it.** Decide if pupils' judgements are realistic. For self-assessment to work well, pupils need to be successful much more often than unsuccessful.

5   **Agree targets.** Use pupils' response to help them set their own individual targets or goals. Of course, they will need guidance, but try to give them as much ownership of the decision making process as possible.

6   **Make a record sheet for the pupils to complete.** Design an easy way for them to record these targets and when they achieve them. This could be stick-on pictures, tick boxes or simple responses to specific questions.

7   **Remind them of the targets.** They will need reminding, and the initial steps will need to be SMART (Small, Measurable, Achievable, Realistic Targets).

8   **Help pupils to decide success.** Get them to assess and record when they have achieved their targets. This may take a little guidance and support, but children should soon get into the idea.

9   **Did they get it right?** Evaluate how accurate you think their judgements are. You can share your impressions with them if you think it will be helpful. Otherwise, just keep your judgements in mind the next time you go through the process.

10 **Continue the process.** Continue this as a cycle of target setting and evaluation. Evidence suggests that the more these systems of self-initiated learning are used, the more children's attainment across the curriculum improves. It also suggests that ICT is perhaps the most appropriate area of the curriculum for self-initiated learning because there are so few boundaries in, say, a multimedia authoring package like 'HyperStudio' (Roger Wagner) or once a computer is linked to the Internet.

33

Keeping and using effective records

An enormous amount of time and energy is spent on record keeping in primary schools, especially around the time of OFSTED inspections. This can only be justified if it improves the quality of teaching in a school and, therefore, the quality of learning of the pupils. The following suggestions may help you to ensure that the records you keep are useful ones.

1   **Do as little as you can get away with** – remember the KISS principle: keep it simple, succinct.

2   **Examples of work will jog your memory when it comes to report writing.** So it is worth collecting work into a usable form when it is completed. You will not have time to trawl through files, floppy disks and hard drives looking for some work which exemplifies a particular skill at report writing time.

3   **If you are going to *use* it, it is worth spending more time on it.** Most records are never *read* by anyone at all. Many are *looked* at by heads and OFSTED, for example, but that barely justifies the time most of them took to compile. However, if you are doing it for your own benefit, and for the benefit of your pupils, then that is a different matter. With any luck, your records will serve a dual purpose.

4   **If it might benefit the pupils, it needs to be accurate.** If you know the next teacher will use the records you send on, then it's worth making sure that the records will be useful. It may be worth while to sit down with the colleague concerned and ask what they would find useful. The chances are that what they want to know will be pretty much the same as what you want to know yourself.

5   **Keep your records concise enough to be useful.** Records for the next teacher should summarize what you did, and where the pupils got to, in no more than three broad groups. Consider how much *you* have read of the records you were given by the last teacher your class had. That will give you a pretty clear indication of what is (and what is not) useful.

6   **Make class and group lists on a computer.** The spin-offs for helping you to work more efficiently are incredible. Once a list has been compiled, get it photocopied. The list can be easily adapted to fit in with different grouping arrangements. Lists done on a spreadsheet can be easily adapted and they can be used in databases, say for Records of Achievement or reports.

7   **Record what pupils did, how much help they needed, and whether they achieved the learning outcome.** As briefly as you can, these are the bare minimum, but probably contain every piece of information relevant to you. A template file created on a computer may help, or a sheet with a series of statements against which you can record the individual level of each pupil will save some time.

8   **Records should reflect what you planned.** If you include details about what the task was, how it was carried out and what was achieved, you should be able to compile a systematic account of progress across the year.

9   **Consider a format you can share with parents and pupils.** Both will read at least some of the entries, so someone will be using it! Obviously, there may be things that you want to have recorded that are not phrased in a way that is fit for parental consumption, so exercise caution. The format you use should also ensure that parents and children do not see information about another child.

10 **Be efficient.** Time and energy spent on record keeping means you have less time to spend on planning and preparing activities, and less energy for teaching. Records are useful, but whether they are essential or not is a matter of personal choice (or conscience).

Chapter 7   Managing ICT in Primary Schools

Managing ICT within the primary school is complex and time consuming for a whole variety of reasons. ICT coordinators act as technicians, trainers, researchers, liaison agents with outside agencies as well as curriculum developers and class teachers. Added to this situation, many coordinators may feel insecure about their own IT skills, let alone their ability to teach and train others to teach what is a complex and rapidly changing area of the curriculum.

In this chapter we offer advice and practical solutions to a range of issues and problems that are part and parcel of coordinating IT in primary schools.

34

The role of the coordinator

Many experienced IT coordinators will tell you that coordinating ICT is impossible. This is certainly true if you have high expectations and slightly more determination than is healthy! But it is not true to say that it is impossible to make a difference, to encourage people to adapt, change and to make progress. The trick is to keep things realistic and manageable. Here are some ways to tackle the task.

1   **Keep an overview of what is going on.** An important aspect is to keep an eye on what is going on in ICT within your school. Knowing what is working well, and what is in need of development, is the only way to use your time effectively, and the only way of planning for the development of your curriculum area.

2   **Remember that IT coordinators are not technicians.** Despite the fact that most IT coordinators are not necessarily qualified to fix hardware and software problems, this is what they can spend much of their time doing. Nobody would ask the language coordinator to stick a cover back on to a damaged reading book, so why should anybody ask an IT coordinator to replace a damaged disk or check a fuse?

3   **Set up systems that take some of the burden from you.** Deflect requests for technical support by setting up systems that support colleagues and reduce the burden on you. Try to make sure staff have access to, and are aware of the existence of, consumable resources. Try to encourage staff to check the obvious things *before* calling for your assistance. Maybe you could draw up a list of common problems and solutions for each member of staff. Get them to write down the details of the problem, so you know what to tell the real technician when you call for assistance. Can the secretary ring on your behalf – eliminating you from the repair process almost completely?

4   **Monitor work and results.** The chances are that you will have a pretty good idea of what is going on in ICT in your school by the questions you get asked or the problems you may be asked to sort out (see tip 2!). It may well be the case that if nobody is asking for your assistance then nobody is using ICT.

5   **Keep track of resources.** To save time, you may want your colleagues to have easy access to ICT resources, but this takes a little organization. Try to keep a catalogue of software that is available in school. One easy way is to use suppliers' product descriptions in their catalogues. Just type them out or cut out the actual adverts and stick them into a catalogue of your own. As far as consumable resources go, it may be best to allocate each teacher a share, but try to make it as generous as possible – you don't want to stifle creativity now, do you?

6   **Steer the curriculum.** Every coordinator has a responsibility for ensuring that their area of the curriculum stays on track. What you want to achieve and how you hope to achieve it will probably be set out in your school's improvement plan. But putting policy into practice may need some careful negotiation, both to attract support in terms of time and finance as well as essential support from your colleagues.

7   **Advise.** Most heads listen to their ICT coordinators! This is partly due to the fact that many heads lack confidence in their own ICT skills as much as any other teacher, and because ICT is becoming an increasingly important area of the curriculum. Your colleagues will also need your help and advice. The difference is that you may need to take your advice to your head (because they know it is going to cost them!), whereas other teachers will undoubtedly come looking for you of their own free will!

8   **Train.** It is more than likely that, as ICT coordinator, you will be called upon to provide both formal and informal training for your colleagues. There is a fine line to be drawn between helping someone develop new skills, and helping to confirm their suspicion that all this technology stuff is more bother than it's worth. (See 'Offering INSET' in the next chapter.)

9   **Get trained.** Try to make sure that your training is relevant. It is likely that opportunities for training in various aspects of teaching and coordinating ICT will present themselves. Many can be ignored simply on the grounds of cost, others may appear to be of no interest to you, but that is not to say that others wouldn't benefit. It is often the case that the very person who should *not* be put forward to attend ICT training is the IT coordinator. Consider whether courses might be useful for others and

be creative in using them to take the burden of attending training programmes from you. For instance, if another member of staff attends a course on say, 'Music in ICT', can they be persuaded to pass on some of what they learn to others?

10   **Remember that less is more!** It is tempting to go out and do it all yourself, but it is possible that all you will achieve is the development of your own skills and the stagnation of everyone else's. Try instead to encourage the use of ICT, and be there to help your colleagues. If you can support their learning and encourage them to develop their own skills through making resources, developing activities, building confidence, you can be sure that their classroom practice will feel the benefit, too.

35

Raising additional funds
(or 'Getting more money out of the head')

Many schools may delegate a budget to the ICT department, but this is usually a subsistence budget intended for use in keeping software up to date, buying consumable resources, and so on. It probably won't be enough to allow for significant development or change, even though these kinds of changes are inevitable. So – remove cap, tug forelock, lay prostrate in front of the head and agree to yard duties for a month if… But if that doesn't appeal, try some of the following!

1   **Get used to the fact that you will never have enough money.** The pace of change and 'progress' in ICT, and especially within ICT in education, means that what you can afford and what you could use will always be poles apart.

2   **Set your priorities out clearly.** Although this isn't about additional funding, it is about making the best of the opportunities you have got. You are bound to have a load of ideas that never get off the ground through lack of time, resources or money, so go for the stuff that you need, or can get real value from, keeping the rest as a wish list!

3   **Build a watertight case.** And present it well. Once you know what you want, put forward your case. Say what you want, what the possibilities are, how well it could be used, what the benefits will be for pupils, what the benefits will be for colleagues, and only then say how much it is.

4   **Remember, you may have the upper hand.** It is still the case that many headteachers look to their ICT coordinators for advice because they feel that they lack specific knowledge of their own in the area. If they think you may know more than they do, they are more likely to be sympathetic to your suggestions. And even if this isn't the case, it'll do your confidence no end of good if you can convince yourself it is!

5   **Remember that people expect ICT to be expensive.** People who hold
    the purse strings often expect ICT to be expensive and they forget that
    the price for equipment that was cutting edge technology last year, drops
    very quickly once it has been superseded by this year's version. When
    things aren't as expensive as they expected, it comes as a pleasant surprise,
    which is more strength to your elbow!

6   **Try to be creative.** Your head will have a variety of sources of funding to
    dip into. It might be worth suggesting that, 'The PTA might like to help
    us out with...' or, towards the end of the financial year, reminding the
    head that parts of some budgets (training, supply cover, and so on) may
    not have been spent. Can you help them out by spending their money for
    them? Keep your eyes open for opportunities to make bids to the LEA or
    the private sector, see your head about helping you put a bid together.

7   **Make the most of voucher schemes.** Voucher schemes for computers and
    other ICT equipment are a potential gold mine. With a little encouragement
    parents and the local community can really come up trumps. Try sending
    out letters to remind parents, send slips that people can post through
    their neighbours letter boxes asking for support, set up collection points
    in local stores if they are prepared to help. You could even try striking
    deals with other schools. Try to enlist helpers to set these schemes up and
    aim to keep the ideas and links going year on year – people soon get into
    the habit and are only too happy to help.

8   **Raise the possibility of running a sponsorship scheme.** Try to get local
    businesses and the community involved in helping you to raise money
    for a specific target – say one new multimedia computer. Get someone to
    run a stall at the school fair on the fund's behalf. Encourage local shops to
    sponsor your scheme by paying for a little advertising. Get someone to
    run a raffle for you. Try the old favourites – penny in a bottle, Smartie
    appeals, 100 clubs – anything that might help. It may take a great many
    small steps, but try to keep the momentum going by keeping everyone
    informed, especially the pupils, because their enthusiasm is very infectious
    (or is it just that their enthusiasm is impossible to ignore?).

9   **Raise the possibility of local business partnerships.** Local businesses,
    governors, and so on may be able to establish links that could help your
    department. Larger companies often get rid of outdated equipment which,
    though no longer hot stuff, may still be perfectly usable. A rather out-of-
    date word processor may help you to free up a better machine in your
    school for more sophisticated uses. Often they are more than happy to let
    local schools take on their cast-offs so spread the word, but do take care,
    businesses rarely throw out good stuff!

10   **Include Governors.** In the end, they decide where money gets spent. If you include them in your planning, they may feel more inclined to support those plans.

11   **Buy a National Lottery ticket.** If you hit the jackpot you could always donate a new computer to your *old* class! On the other hand, however…!

36

Surviving inspection

When it comes to inspection it has to be a team effort, but naturally coordinators are going to be especially concerned about their subject areas. The ICT coordinator's job here is as important as any, and perhaps complicated by the fact that some teachers may not be as confident with teaching ICT as they would like to be. You want your school to show ICT at its best, so here are some ways to plan to achieve this.

1   **Stage manage the event.** It may be tempting to think that the inspectors should take you as they find you, but it would be missing an opportunity not to show what you can do. It needn't be too difficult to stage manage a week's work, the following points may give you a few ideas.

2   **Use display to its full advantage.** It is quite possible that you won't be able to show work in every area of ICT in class time. This work may not fit in with the topics you are looking at that week and so on. But displaying work, with a few captions and maybe a few photographs, will clearly demonstrate what has been going on and take some of the pressure off teaching the more complex ICT skills when the inspectors can identify who is pressing the keys!

3   **Start putting together a portfolio of work.** A collection of examples of good work from across your school, with the odd photo or caption to put activities into context, will give a good overview of a whole year's work in ICT and show how skills develop across the school. It is offering evidence that might otherwise be missed by the inspector.

4   **Get your school paperwork up to date.** The inspectors will expect to see your school policy document for IT, the school's scheme of work for IT and the IT coordinator's job description. It's not a bad idea to read them again yourself, so you and they tell the same story to an inspector! A visit is *not* the best time to say all the things you may disagree with in such papers.

5   **Keep your coordinator file up to date.** Prepare a file that documents not only the ICT section of the school improvement plan and the scheme of work, but also a catalogue of available resources, details of orders placed and a diary of the work you have done as coordinator. This can be another valuable source of evidence. You've probably got all the components already, but putting them in a file will help you to be *seen* to be well organized.

6   **Double-check with each member of staff about what they intend to teach.** If you can get colleagues to plan (loosely) ICT work for the week of inspection well in advance, you can cross-check their activities with the scheme of work and make sure that the relevant skills are being developed. In other words, make sure that policy fits practice!

7   **Get the real teaching in at least the week before!** If you must introduce a new idea to the children, do it the week before inspection; that way the messy stuff, when things go wrong, should be out of the way before the inspectors arrive, but the main points will still be relatively fresh in the minds of the children.

8   **Consolidate.** Try to make sure that as much of the work as possible for the week of inspection is familiar to the children *and* the staff. If you concentrate on consolidation tasks, relatively little should go wrong. Leave the flash stuff, with the pupils inserting video clips into the school's web page, to the teachers who are confident enough to deal with complications.

9   **Sing from the same song sheet.** Inspectors will pick up on, and delve deeper into, areas where they get conflicting messages. It may be worth taking a short period of time, say during a staff meeting, to ensure everyone is up to date with developments within the ICT curriculum, to make sure they are all familiar with their section of the scheme of work and they know what is available and where it is.

10   **Stick to real routines.** If the children are used to working in a certain way in ICT, stick to it. Trying out new work habits just in time for OFSTED may well prove counter-productive. If the class are settled into a routine, even if you know there are disadvantages with that way of working, it may still be better to stick with it – if it isn't broken, don't fix it!

11   **Play to your strengths.** If you feel confident with a bit of multimedia authoring, do it! Your colleagues may rather stick to a bit of creative art work or word processing, so let them play it that way. If someone is feeling up to a bit of modelling with a music package, then so much the better but, if not, it is better not to force the issue. Hopefully, with a bit of discussion and cooperation you should be able to find enough to cover a wide range of concepts.

12   **Don't mention anything negative!** If you know there are issues or things in need of attention, these may be outlined in development plans, but don't give them any more publicity than is necessary. If an inspector has a query, answer it as honestly as you can, but try to avoid planting new concerns at the same time.

13   **Finally, be circumspect about embroidering the truth.** Or, if you are going to lie, don't get caught! A running stitch to keep things together is OK, however, most inspectors will see through the suit of new clothes you fabricate for the ICT emperor parading down the corridor.

37

Whole school tracking and development

Developing a clear and consistent approach to teaching ICT across the school and across the curriculum is essential for effective teaching. One of the best ways of doing this is by developing tracking skills. Not only will this help you develop a consistent and progressive ICT curriculum, but it will also help you build a structure that can be easily updated. Ideally, this should be done through staff development, so all those involved can contribute. Realistically, you might get a staff meeting to run the ideas past the other teachers. The following suggestions show how whole school tracking can be approached, using the National Curriculum as operated in England and Wales as an example of a starting point (but the approach lends itself to any predetermined framework or syllabus).

1   **First, sit down with the dear old National Curriculum for IT.** This may not be the most enthralling read you can imagine, but is the only starting place. Using the end of key stage targets as a guide, try to build a four or five stage map of skills development from an assumed minimum ability to where the children need to be by the end of the key stage for each statement. This could take the form:

   • Know that pressing buttons controls a computer/electronic device

   • Be able to type familiar words on a conventional keyboard

   • Be able to build simple sentences using concept keyboards

   • Be able to use the return, space and delete buttons

   and so on…

2   **Categorize skills.** Try putting the skills you have identified into categories such as 'General ICT skills', 'Literacy', 'Numeracy', 'Handling Information', 'Measurement and Control', and so on. This will help you to identify areas of the curriculum that you might use to develop certain skills.

3   **Now try to match skills to year groups.** This should be fairly straight-forward. By simply stating where you think these skills should be developed, most will be largely developmental, just divide them amongst the relevant year groups.

4   **Now match skills to opportunities.** Once you know which skills each year group should attempt to teach, try to develop activities that fit in with topic work or other schemes of work, or simply adapt existing practice in that year group.

5   **Tackle the gaps.** Once you have done all this, gaps in provision will appear. There may be a serious lack of opportunity to develop control technology in Key Stage 1 for instance. These gaps should form the basis of your development planning, but don't worry about them too much in the short term.

6   **Keep everyone informed.** Show the rest of the staff, when you have managed to put together a draft skills development paper and a scheme of work which outlines possible activities, and explain where these activities fit into the rest of the curriculum (ie linked to specific topics or units of work). Their reactions will give you an indication of what is, and what is not, appropriate. They will be able to offer suggestions that enhance provision.

7   **Put together the final scheme.** Incorporating colleagues' ideas, and perhaps addressing one or two of the gaps in provision, put together a scheme of work. It is perfectly reasonable that this scheme of work may be fairly prescriptive, even to the level of describing activities in some detail and providing additional resources. However, this should probably be done with the caveat that, as long as skills are developed as outlined in the Skills Tracking documents, teachers are free to teach IT in any way they like. This way you support the less confident without stifling those who are more confident and prepared to be adventurous.

8   **Try to include as much support as possible.** If you can provide support in an accessible form within the scheme of work, then pressure should be taken off you. Don't ignore the value of little things, like copies of software guides, or even better, brief overviews and guides to important points, a

trouble shooting guide, the odd ready made overlay that came with the concept keyboard that happens to fit in, originals of disks, catalogues of hardware and software and where to find them. It sounds like a great deal of work, but in the long run it should save you a lot of time.

9   **Introduce the scheme formally.** It is no good just handing out the paperwork and assuming your colleagues will take it all on board. Ask for time during a staff meeting or training day to introduce the scheme formally. Give people time to go through the material, and to look at what is most relevant to them. Try to tackle any queries there and then. And...

10 **Explain your plan or timetable for the implementation of the scheme.** If the scheme means that there are major changes to the way people work, you will have to give some idea of how long you expect the implementation of the policy to take (quite possibly two or three years), and how you are going to support its implementation. See the next set of suggestions for further details.

11 **Do not assume that your work ends here.** Your scheme of work is bound to change constantly as new opportunities present themselves and as the tide of technology continues to rise. However, the structure you have developed here means that new opportunities can be fitted into the existing skills development chart, and it may well be just a case of adapting one or two of the activities. As your scheme has flexibility built in, this only really needs to be recorded in standard planning in the short term. Inclusion in the scheme can wait until the next scheduled review.

38

Whole school development plans

The tracking and development of the ICT curriculum as outlined in the previous set of tips may well be the starting point for a longer-term development or improvement plan. But either way, one thing is for sure, in ICT you are never going to be short of something to develop! One of the most stressful things about implementing the ICT curriculum is the very fact that change is constant and inevitable, so managing this situation can be quite a balancing act. The following suggestions may help you to keep your balance!

1   **Take one step at a time.** Trying to make sea changes overnight is usually counter-productive. If you ask people to take on too many new ideas at once, the chances are that they will not cope well and will subsequently go back to doing it the old way. There is nothing wrong with raising general awareness by introducing a load of new ideas, as long as you are only asking each teacher to take away one or maybe two ideas to develop in their classrooms.

2   **Take staff with you.** The pace of change you may want might not be what the rest of the staff want. Progress needs to be negotiated, and only move on when you feel that everyone is ready (just as you would do with your classes).

3   **Give staff opportunities to give you feedback.** If changes are instigated, it is important that teachers have the opportunity to give you feedback about their successes and failures. If done as a whole school staff, then everyone can learn from one another. At the very least, staff should feed back to the ICT coordinator, so that urgent changes can be made.

4   **Allow time to consolidate.** Once the first steps to a change or development have been taken, it is important to allow some time to consolidate new skills, both for the teachers and for the children. Without time to consolidate, many people quickly forget, which rather defeats the point of the exercise.

5   **Try to make time to evaluate the effect of developments on a regular basis.** Even if you have stuck to the four tips above, it does not mean that the work is over. For a new way of working to become part of the way ICT is used within a school, careful monitoring is needed.

6   **Be prepared to review a situation.** Changes may have to be made in the light of your ongoing evaluations. Because your scheme is flexible, slight adaptations or changes should not require major reworking of documentation.

7   **Get SMART.** SMART stands for Small, Measurable, Achievable, Realistic Targets. This way you reduce the possibility of failure or frustration.

8   **Remember that it is not just the aspirations of the ICT coordinator that are important.** Other members of staff may have firm ideas about what is important. You will probably do better to encourage others' involvement, even if that causes a conflict of interests for you. Being an ICT coordinator can be a lonely business, so keep in with everyone if possible.

9   **Try to develop support structures *before* implementing change.** That way, the support structures become part of the new way of working, and are much more likely to be used effectively. It is basically about trying to develop good habits – at least habits that may take the pressure of supporting your colleagues on an individual basis off you!

10 **Finally, don't expect more than your share.** These days every area of the curriculum seems to be a priority. Although there may well be a very strong case to suggest that ICT should have additional time devoted to its development in your school, everyone has their own priorities and they may not match yours. Of course, take opportunities that present themselves, but also take care not to turn others off.

39

Managing (or surviving) change

The world of ICT is a restless and rapidly evolving one. Just as you begin to get comfortable, your little niche changes and you are in danger of becoming extinct. Perhaps the answer is to make sure that you don't get too comfortable in the first place. Instead, try to maintain a comfortable rate of change. Keeping on top of what is going on need not take too much time, but it is certainly the way to make sure that you are not taken by surprise… and don't worry, the paranoia you may feel about being out of date is perfectly normal.

1   **Keep your eye on the ball.** It helps if you remember that the most important thing of all is that you get to where you are going. Your school improvement plan will identify targets for ICT and attainment on other areas of the curriculum. These are your priority and you should only try to take on board the things that will actually help you to achieve your goals, and to achieve them on time!

2   **Read at least one ICT-related magazine a month.** If you can find a periodical specific to ICT in education, so much the better. *The Times Educatioal Supplement* (TES) has a regular section. It may sound like territory you would rather not have to stray into, but it is amazing how much you can pick up from a 15-minute flick through.

3   **Join a local or national organization.** There are a few organizations set up to support and share ideas about ICT in education. Joining a 'computer group' may sound incredibly anorakish but you'll probably find that most of the other members are bearably human!

4   **Bear in mind that it is impossible to be up to date with everything.** No matter how hard you try, becoming an expert in every aspect of ICT is a total unrealistic goal. Prioritize and concentrate on what is most useful and achievable. In any case, Neils Bohr defined an expert as 'a man who has made every mistake, which could be made, in a very narrow field'!

5   **Let the needs of the curriculum dictate change, not changing technology.**
    If you responded to a new technology because it was there, you would be
    doing it for the wrong reasons. It is far more important that you to start to
    think about, say, access to the Internet because you feel sure it can enhance
    teaching and learning in your school, not because everyone else seems to
    be doing it!

6   **Look to government institutions for guidance.** Currently, BECTa and
    the National Grid for Learning project are forcing issues in ICT in British
    schools. The names may change but the basic idea is sure to remain. Take
    time to look at what they have to say, they usually manage to give a
    reasonable amount of notice. If you have access to the WWW, visit their
    web sites, they are actually more helpful than you might expect. Others
    worthy of a visit include the BBC Education web site and local e-mail
    groups (see Appendix 3).

7   **Decide what is appropriate.** Before deciding whether a new opportunity
    is worth undertaking, consider if it will complement the work you are
    already doing, or whether it will actually cut across the existing curriculum
    or even render parts of it irrelevant. Don't do it because it seems like a
    good idea, do it because it fits.

8   **Consider who is going to do it.** Before going ahead with a new project,
    consider which member of staff will be doing the actual teaching. Are
    they capable? Are they willing? Don't get yourself into a situation where
    you have to provide too much additional support to get a new idea off
    the ground, unless you have backing from the management (backing as
    in teaching cover!).

9   **Consider how you can bring about change.** Sometimes small changes
    and adaptations simply don't achieve the desired results. Throughout
    we have urged caution and tried to encourage taking things one step at a
    time, but if things aren't changing, more radical ideas may need to be
    considered. For instance, moving from a computer in each room to a room
    with all the computers in, providing a dedicated ICT resource – timetabled
    for use by the whole school – might give teachers the time and opportunity
    to really get their teeth into it.

10 **Don't take it all too literally.** There is a good deal of hype about ICT,
    largely forced by computer manufacturers and software developers.
    Someone may try to convince you that their way is the future, but take a
    couple of steps back and wait for things to unfold. If they were right, at
    least you have the opportunity to be just behind the cutting edge!

11 **Don't take it all too seriously.** If you take it seriously, and expect others to do the same, it's never going to be any fun. Working in the world of ICT is serious enough already, so if you put pressure on yourself and on to others, it may make success and progress even less likely.

Chapter 8 Resources for the Implementation of ICT

Getting hold of the resources to facilitate the effective teaching of IT is far from an easy task. Tight budgets, rapidly changing needs and possibilities, and the terrifying rate of perceived obsolescence make keeping pace and getting the best from the equipment you have, quite a juggling act. Add to this the fact that many schools operate a variety of different hardware, operating systems and, therefore, software, it becomes clear that where resources are sited and how they are used is an issue that will continually plague any ICT coordinator.

In this chapter, we offer advice on the sorts of issues that need to be addressed, and some practical advice on how these issues can be tackled.

40 Access to equipment (for children)
41 Organization of resources
42 Effective continuity and progression
43 Helping to ensure compatibility and consistency
44 Offering INSET
45 Disseminating information

40

Access to equipment (for children)

It is good practice in any curriculum area to make sure that children have access to the equipment they need and to the routines associated with the use of that equipment. A disproportionate amount of money is spent on ICT hardware and software in any school where provision is reasonable and, therefore, it is important to try to get the best out of what you have.

1   **Be creative in the management and organization of resources.** For instance, there may be situations or activities in your classroom that realistically require access to more than one computer. Could you arrange to use another class's machine while they are in PE, and can they use yours when you are out of the room?

2   **Consider establishing a cluster.** By arranging some computers and other hardware in one area you might be able to provide better access for everyone in the long run. You will probably need draw up a timetable so that people can plan what to do and know when they are going to be able to do it. It also pays to have times when no one class has priority, and the equipment can be used on an *ad hoc* basis.

3   **Can you implement an open access policy?** Consider whether it would be possible to provide access to ICT equipment during break times, and so on. If you run activities such as curriculum-based projects, making a school newspaper or magazine, setting up a web site with older children, where access to equipment is either highly beneficial or essential, open access is the only way to ensure success. Plus, it's worth loads of OFSTED brownie points!

4   **Ensure children have appropriate physical access.** It may sound obvious, but surprisingly often ignored, that the heights of chairs and computer trolleys should match each other and the children using them. There is

108

much debate about the ergonomics of computer equipment within the private sector, and not without good reason. Just tilting the screen to a better angle can help!

5 **Keep monitors and keyboards close together.** There is some evidence to suggest that the physical relationship between a computer keyboard and its monitor has a significant effect on both the speed and accuracy of pupils' work. Basically, the further children have to switch their gaze between keyboard and screen, the slower and less accurate their work tends to be. Perhaps laptops and palmtops may be better for young children after all!

6 **Maximize!** If opportunities to purchase new equipment come along, think carefully about what will provide the best value for money. Palmtop computers are becoming increasingly sophisticated and easier to use, and you can buy five of them for the same price as a new desktop machine. There is plenty that they can't do, but consider the possibilities before committing hard won funding.

7 **Consider whether access to the Internet is really worth while.** Establishing new links to the Internet can be an expensive business. It is important to consider whether one new line can really have an impact. Even with cheap local calls, you aren't going to want to have a computer hooked up permanently to the WWW, and without that level of access it might not be worth while. There are ways of using Internet services without actually being connected all the time. These include e-mail, off-line browsing, printouts of information and others, such as video conferencing that require relatively short periods of time on-line. The message is don't bother arranging access to something you won't be able to use efficiently.

8 **Maintain easy access to software.** If you can manage to set up every computer so that it has access to the same software (either stored on hard disk or with a standard collection of floppy disks), you can maintain equality of access and...

9 **Remember that floppy disks give universal access.** You may be able to make more efficient use of the computer equipment you have by using floppy disks to store children's work. If children have their own disks, with copies of all their own work, providing each computer has appropriate software, they may be able to go and work on someone else's machine. Of course, if you have a network, this problem disappears altogether.

10   **Consider how much access is really necessary.** Some ICT activities require sustained access over a long period of time, for example, when children are using computers to collect, store and interrogate information for a science investigation. Other activities really need short but frequent periods of access, perhaps for improving keyboard skills or mental agility using a drill and practice program. Keep this in mind when you are trying to set up systems to provide appropriate access.

41

Organization of resources

Where resources are stored and how they are organized will have a significant impact on how they are used. It will be up to the coordinator to establish and maintain routines and procedures for the use and organization of equipment.

1   **Keep organization as simple as possible.** For your own sake, as well as that of your colleagues, try to keep organizational procedures as simple as possible. For one thing, simple ideas tend to work the best and, secondly, if they are too complex, people will simply ignore them and do it the easy way anyway!

2   **Organize your equipment to maximize its potential.** Putting the majority of your computer hardware into one, dedicated resource centre may be the best way of using it to its full potential. Alternatively, perhaps a more flexible approach will suit your school better. One thing is for sure, if you have one computer in one classroom, especially if it is shared with other classes on a rotational basis, the chance of that computer being used to its full potential is low.

3   **Organize less fundamental resources centrally.** Equipment such as floor robots, sensing equipment, control boxes, and so on should be held in a single, central area if possible. Choose an area where everyone knows what is available and where it is. You may need to circulate information about these resources, and a gentle reminder and update every year or so won't go amiss.

4   **Target software.** Partly due to the higher costs of site licences as well as the need to ensure progression, it is a good idea to target software to appropriate age groups and teachers. A few good programs, well placed within the curriculum and in relation to individual teacher's skills and experience, tends to be far more productive than simply providing a wide range of software in the hope that the children will learn through bombardment.

5 **Old equipment may still be useful.** Just because a piece of equipment is old, it doesn't mean that it can't enhance the ICT curriculum. Even if an old computer is only used for keyboard skills or developing redrafting, number crunching, or even role play – if there is room for it, it is worth keeping.

6 **Give teachers access to consumable resources.** Dishing out new ink cartridges or replacing floppy disks is unnecessarily time consuming for an ICT coordinator. Try to set up a system that gives teachers access to these resources, but makes them responsible for preserving stocks, too. Just signing out new stock can add the required measure of guilt that ensures people don't take advantage. Remember it is not your job!

7 **Provide staff with as much information as possible.** The more information they have about what is available and where it is, the less they will have to bother you about it. Of course, there is also the old adage to consider, 'You can lead a horse to water, but you can't make him drink'. Don't expect everyone to use the systems you set up, and try not to condemn them for it either!

8 **Consider what others can do to help.** Try to keep resources accessible to both teachers and pupils. Label everything and encourage the use of whatever systems you feel are necessary. You may well find that the children are a lot better at sticking to the procedures than your colleagues are!

9 **Provide 'hands-on' access.** As a general rule, what people have to go and look for, won't get used! If possible, try to make sure that the resources that each year group *really* need are to hand. Where certain resources have to be passed around, try to arrange for these resources to be delivered to the people who should need them next. If nothing else, this will provide a gentle reminder.

10 **Communicate!** This means communicate in both directions – talk and listen. Keep your colleagues informed about what is where, but also try to set up procedures that allow them to pass on information about problems, or ideas to make life easier for them, too. If you have a cluster of machines, it is a good idea to keep a log of what goes wrong, so that busy teachers can pass on relevant information without having to spend hours tracking down the coordinator!

42

Effective continuity and progression

In ICT, time is short and ensuring effective continuity and progression will be another important factor in maximizing the impact that ICT can have on your schools curriculum. (See also our section on Whole School Tracking and Development in Chapter 7.) Here are some starters for continuity and progression.

1 **Put skills first.** If you look at all ICT work from the point of view of developing ICT specific skills (and hopefully supporting various other skills from across the whole curriculum into the bargain), it is easier to ensure that what you teach in each year group will build upon work done in the previous year. Map out what ICT skills you think should be developed and when, and use this as the basis for all your school's ICT planning.

2 **Make sure that statements of intent are clear and concise.** If you have mapped skills across your school as outlined in the section on Whole School Tracking and Development in Chapter 7, try to make sure that the statements you use are clear and unambiguous. Don't be afraid of making it sound like an idiot's guide, the clearer such descriptions are the less likely repetition and misinterpretation become, and that means that time is spent constructively.

3 **Target the use of content-free or generic software.** It is tempting to try out lots of different word processing or desktop publishing packages because they all promise so much in their advertising. But if every year group has a new package to get to grips with it can slow down their learning. With a bit of research and discussion, you should be able to get just two packages that will do the job: one for Early Years and Key Stage 1 and possibly another for Key Stage 2.

4   **Disseminate information.** It is important to make sure that everyone
     knows, in broad terms, what everyone else is doing. Your scheme of work
     should map what happens, and where, in reasonable detail. Use this as a
     focus for introducing ICT across the school and across the curriculum.
     The more others know about what is going on, the less likely you are to
     come across repeated activities or to miss out important concepts.

5   **Assess to ensure continuity and progression.** Although formal
     assessment of ICT is not statutory currently, it is likely to be before long.
     But whether it is or it isn't, assessing abilities has many advantages for
     ICT. It should be kept simple but formal, and will indicate whether skills
     are being developed at appropriate levels (is your scheme of work
     realistic?) and whether activities are developing relevant skills.

6   **Make sure records are passed on.** If you have formal planning and
     assessment procedures in place in your school, it might be a good idea to
     ask if you can collect the ICT relevant paperwork and pass it on to the
     next teacher. This will also give you an opportunity to develop a better
     overview of what is (and what is not) working out.

7   **Encourage display of ICT work.** If the work that is done in each year
     group is regularly displayed, other teachers will have clear ideas of what
     is going on; this should give a good indication of the level they should
     probably be working at, too. You can then use some of it to…

8   **Compile a portfolio of work.** As with displays, this can provide a good
     indication of what can be achieved and where it can be achieved. It will
     also help disseminate good ideas and effective practice. This work may
     not need to be assessed, but include a brief description of purpose of the
     task and the level of support offered to put the work into context anyway.

9   **Get staff to share their successes and failures.** More than likely, staff in
     your school will already spend more than enough time in meetings and
     you don't want to make this situation worse, but it may be a good idea to
     encourage, where appropriate, the sharing of good ideas and of heroic
     failures, a kind of 'show and tell' for ICT.

10   **Take colleagues' concerns seriously.** You may face quite a few road blocks
     to your plans. These road blocks are usually put up because activities
     require unrealistic expectations of your colleagues' own skills, or present
     real classroom management issues. There is no point just hoping to avoid
     these issues, and if work isn't being undertaken, then continuity and
     progression doesn't really have a chance.

43

Helping to ensure compatibility and consistency

(or, where to get help when your dongle and your display don't want to play)

ICT coordinators might find themselves faced with a range of different hardware, operating systems and software that they have to maintain, support and weave into a coherent and effective scheme of work. Without detailed knowledge of each different platform this can be very difficult, although many basic ideas are transferable. If you already have that detailed working knowledge, you will manage but, if not, there are plenty of people who should be able to help.

1 **Unless you know – ask.** There are a great many people who have it in their best interests to keep you informed, particularly service agents and suppliers who want you to be happy with what they do, and to have little if any reason to come back and complain. So, don't be afraid to ask for their help and advice.

2 **Hold suppliers to their advice.** When ordering new hardware or software, explain in some detail what you want to do and how you want to do it. Make sure you get them to confirm that what you want to do is achievable with the product they are offering to supply, and hold them to their promises if it doesn't, or if it doesn't do it very well.

3 **Get help from your local ICT centre.** That's what they are there for, to give you help and advice and to ensure that what you want to do is achievable, and that it is achievable with the hardware and software you have access to.

4   **Remember that this is one of the things the WWW does best.** Virtually every ICT supplier or manufacturer has a web site these days. If you have access to the Internet, visit relevant sites, which often have highly detailed product specifications that run to several printed pages. The downside is that these are usually written in Martian, or at least modern geek, but it is useful to have these details to hand so that you can check your approximate translation with a supplier or help-line assistant by old-fashioned methods of communication, such as the telephone and voice.

5   **Get in touch with suppliers' teacher support services.** Once more, that is what they are there for, and if they can't answer specific queries they will know where to look. Sometimes this may be a matter of giving you a useful phone number, other times they will get back to you with the information you need.

6   **Get together with other ICT coordinators in your area.** Meetings of such people are bound to happen once in a while, so try to go along. It is quite amazing how many irritating problems (ICT related, naturally) you will have in common, but also how many simple solutions you will come away with. Only other ICT coordinators know how it feels – these situations are definitely the most productive, even if they only confirm that you are not alone!

7   **Get on to feeder schools.** Secondary or high schools tend to have access to staff who specialize in ICT and it is in their interests to help you out because, in their heart of hearts, they know where the *real* ICT teaching goes on and they don't want to do it if they can get you to do it first.

8   **Contact your local college or university.** They will certainly have someone with technical expertise, particularly with e-mail and the web. They may even be happy to 'adopt' you.

9   **Ask to see new hardware and software working.** Before splashing out on new hardware or expensive software, ask for a free trial. Many software developers and suppliers now do this as a matter of course; hardware is a different ball game. As likely as not, the onus will be on you to go and see it working. If this is impossible, make sure you have some sort of comeback if what you order doesn't do what you stipulated. (And don't get complacent, we all get caught out on this one from time to time.)

10   **Don't just accept one point of view.** It is always worth double-checking information with different suppliers. It is amazing how often you will get conflicting information and advice, so it is sometimes necessary to talk to the 'technical department', too.

11   **Accept that it is an unwinnable battle.** No matter how hard you work at it, technology marches on too quickly and, more often than not, is irritatingly unconcerned with backwards compatibility (geek for 'No of course your old program/machine won't run [on] our wonderful new program/machine', accompanied or preceded by a slow sucking in of breath over teeth). Some manufacturers are a lot better than others (notably Apple, believe it or not. A six-year-old Mac will still run most modern software, given enough RAM and a bit more waiting around!).

44

Offering INSET

All primary school teachers are now expected not only to be teachers, but also to be trainers for their colleagues. As the ICT expert you will probably find yourself in the position of offering training more often than most, both formally and informally. Even if you feel far from qualified it will still be your responsibility. Here are some short cuts.

1 **Identify training needs.** You can do this yourself, based on how you feel things are going in ICT or through a curriculum audit, but probably the best and least threatening way is through the school improvement plan. If your school has one that is readable, get hold of it and see if your curriculum area is, or contains, an area that is in need of attention. When helping to put together new improvement plans, try to identify a realistic number of such areas in need of attention.

2 **Don't rush in!** Once you think you have established a training need, it might be tempting to go ahead and organize some INSET, but it might be worth taking a step back and considering why this need has arisen. It could be that a lack of resources is more to blame, or it could be that there is a lack of progression and problems are being experienced because the ground work is not being done effectively. Changes in staffing, sickness, unfamiliarity with resources, inconsistent interpretation of attainment targets and so on, could all be sources of the problem, and so training needs could need careful consideration.

3 **Do you have to do it yourself?** If the problem seems to be limited to a small number of staff or a single, isolated problem, you might be able to tackle it effectively by yourself, but if it is a more complex issue why not ask if you can invite your LEA adviser in to see if they can offer a fresh perspective?

4   **If you think you can do it yourself, try not to get carried away.** Set yourself very specific and achievable targets. How much work you do to support staff in attaining those targets is up to you, but write a specific brief and tell the staff exactly what you intend to offer them before you start. This will help to keep everything clearly focused.

5   **If you are approached to offer training, make sure you are set specific targets.** If your head wants you to run a training day, make sure you get them to write a clear brief about what they want you to do. Once they have set those targets, it may be worth discussing the feasibility of these targets and how you might go about tackling them.

6   **Then, ask for time to get ready.** Arranging whole staff INSET is a very time consuming job and many school managers would try to give their staff time to arrange it. However, if the offer isn't forthcoming, set out what you think you will have to do and approach your headteacher with your proposals. Once they see what is involved they may be even more sympathetic.

7   **Most of the INSET you offer will be one-to-one.** Simply because most ICT-related training is about specific problems that arise during the normal teaching day, colleagues are bound to approach you for a quick fix! Keep a note of what you do as a demonstration of what you have done in your curriculum area.

8   **Ask if you can tackle recurring issues with the whole staff.** If the same problems arise regularly, it might be worth considering a whole staff training event. At least it will help you avoid repeating yourself too often.

9   **Don't try to tell people too much at once.** This is especially true at the end of the day, so try to provide notes and visual prompts about what you are talking about. Many are happy if they just have something to take away with them that looks nice and acts as a memory jogger.

10   **Make it practical.** Listening to one person for an hour or so gets boring. Practical activities are easier to remember and often make more sense. They tend to be more fun and people have an opportunity to do exactly what they would try to do in the classroom.

45

Disseminating information

In the interests of promoting debate and good ideas, it is important to try to share as much information as possible. How you go about this will have a significant impact on how useful this information will be to your colleagues and, ultimately, the children. Here are some principles for productive dissemination.

1   **Be brief.** Information needs to be useful and accessible, otherwise colleagues probably won't have the time to go through it all. Brevity is certainly an art!

2   **Disseminate information about courses yourself.** Even if you do not go on the course, it is important that you get feedback from the person who did, and then pass that information on to colleagues yourself. This way you can put what was discussed into an appropriate form for use in your school.

3   **Keep colleagues up to date.** This is especially important when you manage to get hold of new resources. A brief description of new hardware and software is useful to allow others to make informed decisions about what they want to have a look at. One easy way of doing this is to cut out, or copy product descriptions from catalogues.

4   **Grab time where you can.** Taking five minutes at the end of a staff meeting (or preferably at the beginning of a staff meeting) to go through new information is far more effective than distributing a couple of pages of notes and expecting your colleagues to get around to reading them, let alone making sense of them.

5   **Set up a 'Show and Tell' session of your own.** For those who are interested to see first hand what the list of apparently unconnected statements on a handout are really all about, offer a time, probably after school, to do a quick demonstration.

6 **Target your audience.** If a new resource or idea for effective teaching strategies, activities, and so on is not appropriate for everyone, try to target your audience. Attending Key Stage or departmental meetings may be an effective way of doing this.

7 **Get parents and governors involved**. See if you can get members of the school community to contribute by bringing in ideas from home. Find out what the children do at home and see if it can be woven into school work.

8 **Shout about your successes.** Encourage everyone to share the good experiences. If they let you know, it might be possible for you to build these ideas into your training, or to introduce the ideas at staff meetings and get the teacher concerned to describe what went on.

9 **Share ideas with the whole education community.** Organizations such as MAPE, magazines such as *Child Education* or, less ambitiously, your ICT centre's newsletter are all places where you can share your ideas and get others' ideas about good practice.

10 **Get connected to an appropriate e-mail bulletin board.** If you have Internet access, try to get on to an education bulletin board once in a while. This is a way of sharing your ideas and receiving others in return. The SENCO forum for special needs is particularly good.

Chapter 9   Supporting Colleagues

A subheading for this chapter could be, 'You can lead a horse to water but you can't make it drink'. It can be a very frustrating business being an IT coordinator. It takes hours of effort to organize and manage IT and now ICT, to develop imaginative and worthwhile activities and the resources to help implement these activities. And there are hours of research into appropriate software, and into how to get the best out of an all too limited budget, only to see computers sitting in corners gathering dust or covered with a cloth and acting as plant stands. There never seems to be enough time to help your colleagues to make the most of the opportunities they have.

In this chapter we try to offer practical help and advice on how to manage your time as an IT coordinator, on how to offer valuable support for your colleagues and on how to promote what you want to achieve without turning everyone else off!

46

Supporting colleagues in their teaching of IT

IT is part of the curriculum teachers must deliver. However, as it is not (yet) assessed formally like other subjects, it is easy for it to be ignored at worst, or receive a lower priority at best. Any system of support must be an evolutionary process. The things that work survive and develop, things that don't quickly become extinct! Here are some thoughts on how to approach supporting your colleagues' teaching.

1   **Develop a common approach.** This will need to be with the agreement of other staff. You may be better off compromising and using someone else's perhaps more universally accepted suggestions, than steamrollering your ideas through. Your development should also reflect the school's current priorities, so that IT work supports work in other curriculum areas.

2   **Create support packs for the programs you want them to use.** You can encourage the use of particular programs by putting your effort into supporting them. Try a guide on the basic word processor to start with. Or how to combine text and graphics. This support can be quite brief, from a prompt card, which you can build up into a support pack relevant to your school's scheme of work. Can you share resources such as these with other teachers? (Try www.editsite.demon.co.uk)

3   **Share effective practice.** A few minutes at the beginning of a staff meeting for a 'show and tell' might be a good way to get going. As IT is cross-curricular, ask for a little bit of time in different INSET sessions. If you get other staff to report on what they are doing this also values their contributions. You may want to consider having a display that draws on a theme in IT which has work from different age groups.

4   **Keep consistency from your scheme of work to your organization of resources.** Organize your software and support materials to reflect your scheme of work. Staff should have a copy of this. It should spell out on a termly basis what is expected. Then the materials, which support the classes they are teaching, should link to this. Support material will then link directly to the scheme of work.

5   **Ask to teach alongside colleagues.** It may be hard to get non-contact time to do this. Asking for one session a term with a specific aim, which fits in with the school's current priorities, may be more successful. It will produce results. The best suggestion is to support pupils the first time, particularly if the teacher is not confident, then support other groups while the teacher works with the ICT activity.

6   **Make a bank of examples of activities.** It is very motivating to see examples of what children have done. Collecting good examples from colleagues also values their contribution. These could initially form an exhibition or display you have coordinated, then the samples of work can be put together in a portfolio. This is useful for OFSTED, too.

7   **Have a 'trouble shooting tips for teachers' page.** This should save you time and effort if you can identify the common problems and help your colleagues to solve them for themselves. You may even get some of your colleagues to help with them. (There are a few ideas that might help with this in the 'If it doesn't work' section in Chapter 12.)

8   **Keep hard drives and desktops organized in similar ways.** As computers get more and more powerful the organization of the different machines needs to be as similar as possible. This will make it easier for pupils and teachers to learn how to find their way around on different machines.

9   **Make a series of changes together.** When you need to update software, try to do several things at once so you can explain what is new to people all together.

10 **Play to their strengths.** It will be easier to interest the art coordinator in some art-related software for example, and they may well get better results from their pupils than you would.

47

Supporting colleagues in their own use of IT

Teachers need to develop their own ICT skills. They will not always achieve this easily. As computers and software become more complex, staff need even more time to become familiar with the basics before they can begin to see the possibilities. Here are some ways you can help your colleagues.

1   **Establish open access for staff.** The biggest problem is giving staff enough time on the equipment. Considering how you can get them to use computers more is one of the IT coordinator's biggest challenges. Be creative…

2   **Loan equipment over holidays.** There are difficulties with this, particularly insurance cover, and there is no doubt that connection leads suffer when continually connected and disconnected. However, it is more important that equipment is used as much as possible.

3   **Encourage them to play.** One of the major differences between adult and child learners at the computer is that children play. Adults frequently want to know what to do before they do it. They will wait until they think they will get it right before they will do anything. With computers there is often more that one way to do things, and it is important to learn and find out things for yourself.

4   **Don't get upset when equipment breaks down or it goes wrong.** At least the equipment was being used! The only thing you can be sure of is that it *will* go wrong, but an overreaction on your part compounds the problem – people are already frightened enough of computers!

5   **Make resources you have made available on disk.** It is easier to alter a help sheet or task card that someone else has created than start from scratch. Distributing ideas on paper and templates on disk is a considerable

help. It is also beneficial to have a clean copy from which to make replacements for the chewed versions from time to time.

6   **Ask for copies of colleagues' resources on disk to distribute.** This has the advantages of valuing colleagues' contributions *and* decreasing what you have to do! (Try www.editsite.demon.co.uk)

7   **Get them to tutor each other as 'experts'.** As with pupils, in peer tutoring for adults it is often easier to learn from someone who is just a little further ahead in skills and knowledge than from an expert, especially if the expert is on hand to offer supplementary advice when needed.

8   **Have planning and assessment forms on disk.** Again it is easier to start from something someone else has done, but if you can encourage colleagues to use computers to type reports, produce letters to parents, organize their planning, records and so on, then you are promoting the use of ICT in perhaps the most useful way!

9   **Supply class lists on disk.** This could even be established as an administrative job rather than one for the IT coordinator. Management will love it if there is a spreadsheet file and a prepared blank database of pupils that they, and the other teachers, have access to!

10 **Set up label formats for equipment and displays on the computer.** This will encourage staff to use the computers routinely. Templates or stationery files for drawer and shelf labels will get used. Labels for pupils' work for display can be used by the pupils as well as by teachers!

11 **Encourage colleagues to get their own computers.** Research proves that teachers' skills really only develop when they have a computer at home and use it for their school work. There is not enough time in the school day to learn to use ICT skills on top of hearing readers, play duty, displays, photocopying…!

12 **Look out for second-hand equipment bargains for staff to buy.** New models of computers are expensive. Many of the programs teachers would want to use do not need the latest model with hyperspeed chips and ultrabyte hard drives. Some companies even specialize in reconditioned equipment or 'pre-enjoyed' machines. Why not stick the odd advert you come across onto the staff room notice board?

13 **Tape video programmes for staff or buy a distance learning package.** The BBC, Channel 4, NCET/BECTa and the Open University all produce materials that can be taped or bought at reasonable cost.

48

Providing access to resources and equipment

Staff need to use equipment if they are to become familiar with it. Instructions for using equipment need to be easy to find and to follow. The key to getting staff to use the equipment is to make it easy and useful to use! Keeping material on display or easily accessible is helpful, although such arrangements can easily gather dust. If it isn't used regularly, file it somewhere else and try something different. Here are some ways of whetting colleagues' appetites.

1   **Start with something they will have success with.** This may be just a game to get confidence boosted, or a simple worksheet with a desktop publishing package which they can use. Nothing succeeds like success!

2   **Offer something they will be interested in.** Offer a maths program to the maths coordinator, a new art package to the art coordinator...

3   **Suggest something for holiday play.** When staff borrow the computer for a holiday suggest something they could use (particularly if they have children of their own they can experiment on), *and* suggest they produce a five-point help sheet from it for their class. Give them an example on paper or on disk to get them going. You might be able to show then how to take screen shots ('print screen' to Windows users) to help them make even more eye-catching help sheets.

4   **Support routine, administrative tasks.** See management about making it part of their expectation that some aspects of administrative work are computerized. This needs either to be efficient, or have other beneficial spin-offs. Getting each teacher a class list on disk and a template for a checklist is at least a start.

5   **Consider having a computer and printer in the staff room.** Maybe even arrange this to have Internet access. If you can get a computer and printer

in the staff room it will be used. You may need to provide this if your school expects staff to do planning and record keeping or report writing on computer. Make sure it can be used by pupils at other times, too. You may even get a phone line in the staff room that way, too!

6   **Make sure your site licences let staff use copies of key programs at home.** If you can get compatible software between home and school you will get staff bringing work in from home to use at school.

7   **Consider Internet access for staff when you sign on for your school.** Some Internet providers offer a reduced cost deal which includes evening and weekend access for teachers from home; the 'Internet for Learning' service offered by Research Machines being one example. The National Grid for Learning is expanding rapidly, and will offer a range of resources on-line.

8   **Negotiate a timetable for shared resources.** Again, it needs to be negotiated or it will not be followed. You will also not have enough information to plan the best times for everyone. Some teachers may want to use scarcer resources in a particular term, according to how their other work is planned. Also, with increasing assessment in different years, it may pay to plan how equipment is used to take into consideration when classes will *not* be using it.

9   **Remind staff when their turn for timetabled resources is approaching.** Do this nicely, helpfully, supportively. *Suggest* activities. *Offer* help. Try hard not to appear to be nagging!

10   **Deliver portable timetabled equipment to staff when it is their turn.** If the robot or Roamer arrives at the end of the week before they are due to use it, staff have no excuse – especially if you have reminded them. Nicely of course, helpfully, supportively…

11   **Develop support packs.** These can be stored with termly or thematic resources as appropriate, or can be passed between classes as needed. These should fit clearly with the scheme of work for IT and curriculum plans in other areas.

12   **Have prompts and labels on equipment to remind people of the agreed procedures.** For example, remind colleagues to recharge/remove batteries from floor robots. It is not that people ignore what has been agreed, they just forget or are too busy. A big friendly label to remind them makes it harder to forget; it can also prompt the children who may well be able to carry out many of these tasks.

49

Designing support materials

Support materials are everything from screen wipes to SCSI cables, but focus primarily on helping teachers implement the IT scheme of work effectively, and they are virtually essential if the staff in your school are less than utterly obsessed by the relative benefits of C++ over Java. You can't support your colleagues every minute, but you can try to make sure that some sort of support is available.

1 **Make it manageable.** Be realistic, you can't write help sheets and guides for all the programs regularly used in schools. Find other sources and keep what you intend to do manageable. It is often worth waiting a while before you start writing reams of help sheets. Identify which parts help sheets are needed for and concentrate on those.

2 **Photocopy key parts of manuals.** This is the best place to start. Make an extra copy and keep it as a master. You may find that for some things this is all you need to do.

3 **Print out help menus as they are difficult to use on screen.** It can be frustrating flipping between help notes and a program. Some sections may be particularly valuable and worth printing out. Again keep a clean copy for yourself to save having to print it out all over again. You may even be able to use the text as part of your own help sheets.

4 **Get pupils to write 'top tips' and 'handy hints' sheets.** This is not only time saving for you, and beneficial for the pupils, but also will concentrate on what the users really need.

5 **Keep ideas books and materials on display.** Displays of pupils' work are often the best starting point for getting teachers going. Like any display, it needs to be changed from time to time to prevent it becoming like wallpaper.

6   **Use display to support independent work.** A poster on 'saving and printing' could be placed near the computer.

7   **Support the most used programs first.** Your efforts will be best spent on supporting the most frequently used programs, and addressing the commonest or most persistent problems. Spending hours over a help sheet for a program used once or twice a term is probably not worth the effort, although it can be an excellent way of developing your own knowledge and understanding! If a photocopied section of the manual is insufficient, consider finding an easier program.

8   **See if your local resource centre has a guide or support pack.** This will save you hours! Don't reinvent wheels.

9   **Share resources with other IT coordinators.** You may feel you want to swap rather than give. Best of all is to agree to develop resources as part of a team, and then share them in electronic format so you can alter them to fit your situation.

10   **Keep copies on file.** If you mark master copies with the dot from a highlighter pen, or stick a brightly coloured spot on the corner of each sheet, you stand slightly less chance of losing them.

11   **There is a lot of material for major commercial packages on the Internet.** Doing a search on '[program name] tutorial' or ' help' may yield something useful for little effort. If you do intend to use it – send an e-mail as a courtesy. It is amazing how willing people are to share.

12   **Document how and where to find things.** If notes are to hand, people are more likely to use the computer, but if they can't be there all the time, a signpost may do!

13   **Inform your colleagues and communicate how you think the system is supposed to work.** Don't worry that they will forget. It is also reasonable that they should forget. Your nine-point plan for 'restocking printer cartridges', or your 'A3000 printer troubleshooting flow diagram' may be burnt into *your* consciousness because you poured blood, sweat and tears into it, but it will only impinge peripherally on the awareness of others. Make it easy for them. Have a reminder prompt on files, folders and resource boxes.

14   **Work out how they know where to find things.** If you can't work it out, how will they? Where would *you* look? What needs to be on hand, what needs to be easily accessible, what can be shelved or stored in a cupboard?

50

Providing technical support

The dilemma is between developing independence on the part of your colleagues and offering effective and timely support.

1   **Don't!** 'IT technician' may nearly be an anagram of 'I teach ICT', but you are not a technician. You are not paid to be a technician as well as a teacher. Get someone else to do it. It is not your job, despite what the headteacher thinks. You may have a local authority which can offer technical support. A local secondary school will probably have a technician whose time you could pay for. A commercial company may be prohibitively expensive. Get a quote and shock your headteacher. It is worth repeating, you are *not* a technician, you are *not* a technician (says the pot to the kettle).

2   **Learn from technicians when they are needed, particularly when it is a software problem.** Although you are *not* a technician (see point 1) some problems are easily sorted out and you may decide it is easier to fix them yourself (the pot's excuse!).

3   **Establish a system for support that will work when you are not there.** As the amount of ICT equipment increases in school, it will mean more breakdowns. To survive you must have a system that can function without you, so set it up that way from the beginning.

4   **Have a fault record sheet and log.** This will not only help with individual problems, which the school secretary could phone in, but may also help you identify common or recurring problems more quickly.

5   **When you solve a problem, tell whoever reported it how you sorted it out.** They may be able to solve it themselves next time.

6   **Teach pupils to solve problems.** You will only need to tell *them* how to sort it out *once*! Even better, have a help squad (to ensure equal opportunities try to make sure it has a high proportion of girls in it, balanced racial composition, and so on).

7   **Can anyone else help you?** Try another IT coordinator or support staff at the IT centre. Have any parents expertise (electricians who could make up cables for you)? What about a governor? Is there a local university or college who may be able to sort out difficulties (most higher and further education establishments have been connected to the Internet for longer than schools, and may be able to offer expertise)? Ask the hardware or software supplier or, as a last resort, ring the manufacturer direct.

8   **Make a cup of tea or take along a good novel when you telephone for help.** You will become irritatingly familiar with the electronic version of Mozart's *Eine Kleine Nachtmusik* which seems to be obligatory on help lines! You will be surprised how quickly you get through *War and Peace* as you wait for help.

9   **Never believe *anyone* who says they will ring you back.** Ask for their name and for a time by when they will have got back to you. Write this down and get the school secretary to remind them when they forget, and tell them when you will be available. Try turning the length of time into a challenge or sweepstake for the staff (well, you have to keep smiling!).

10   **Get colleagues to ring for help, too.** This will not only help you, but will make them appreciate what you do. The danger here is that the unenthusiastic will take this as permission not to do anything, so use your judgement.

11   **When all else fails, look in the manual.** Some manuals are actually readable these days, a few even make sense. On very rare occasions, we think you may find something that will fix your problem. We should stress *may*. Really. OK, you guessed it, we are lying. We have *never* solved a problem by reading the manual. However, we do have faith that someone, somewhere must have. Surely. Otherwise why do they write manuals that include a 'troubleshooting' section?

51

Choosing hardware and software

In practice, your choices will be constrained by cost and available budget as well as the advice you can get locally. You may have to follow a local purchasing policy. However, some thought and research before you buy will pay off later. You cannot be an expert in the vast range of equipment and software available, so you will need some strategies to help you decide what to purchase. The following suggestions may help you to build your strategy.

1 **Consider how it will benefit the pupils' learning.** It may help the teachers to be more effective or efficient. However, when resources are scarce the key point must be that the ICT equipment should be directly beneficial to teaching *and* learning.

2 **Hardware purchases should build on the existing skills of staff and pupils.** It may become necessary to undertake a major change of operating system at some point. Do not underestimate the difficulties that this will create. If you decide to change the make of computer and operating system it will certainly slow down, at least initially, the development of pupils' and teachers' ICT skills.

3 **Identify any hidden costs.** These may be simply more cartridges and paper for printers. Internet connections may have many hidden pitfalls. You may find you need headphones to get the best out of sounds from a CD-ROM about musical instruments. You may have to upgrade your machines to get the best from software, and so on.

4 **Get good basic software.** One customizable word processor which can be adapted (through menus, tool bars or palettes) will be enough for a school. A decent integrated package gives you word processing, desktop publishing, drawing, painting, spreadsheets and databases for comparatively little cost. Some now even have a web publishing package included.

5   **Only get what you really need.** It may be nice to have a wonderful spelling program that reports every mistake the pupils make and records their progress. However, they may have been better off learning spellings on bits of card in pairs as a collaborative task for 10 minutes and keeping a record of their progress themselves.

6   **A few good programs are better than boxes of unused disks.** More is not necessarily better. It is difficult to use more than a couple of programs well each term. A few time filler drill and practice programs may be useful on occasions, but they are not worth spending lots of money or time on.

7   **Good software helps pupils become better learners.** Supporting independence, self-checking, identifying and developing strategies, identifying their own improvement, learning transferable skills are the most desirable outcomes from software. The more expensive the equipment or software, the more you should expect from it.

8   **Try before you buy.** Make sure it will work with your equipment. Ask for a demo version or for a rep to show you it working. Try it out at your local IT centre. Go to software exhibitions, look on the web. Ask the supplier to recommend a local school that is using it, which you could ask about how it *really* works. Be critical.

9   **Choose software with built-in help and good manuals.** If it has a teacher's support pack, get that, too. Don't get something that is very complicated to use. You will spend all your time teaching people how to use it. Remember they are unlikely to share your enthusiasm and dedication.

10   **Just because it is on the computer does not mean that it is worth while.** Computers offer some features which are beneficial for teaching. In general you should also be developing pupils' IT capability and ICT skills when they are using the equipment, so as to get the best value from it.

52

Looking after yourself

A primary school teacher's job is never done. You could always do that little bit more. Teaching itself is exhausting and demanding. Having a time consuming extra responsibility such as being an IT coordinator makes the job doubly challenging. You must make time to look after yourself, to help you cope, and to manage stressful situations. Here are some ways of keeping your cool.

1   **Be realistic about what you can do.** Prioritize tasks and set yourself 'done by' dates. Keep a record of what you have done. Files and lists may be boring, but they keep your work organized and can give you a sense of satisfaction, too. A coordinator's file will be useful for inspection, too (and, most likely, will give you a feeling of smug self-satisfaction when your file is three inches – sorry, 7.62 centimetres – thick and every other coordinator's contains about four A4 sheets! One has to get one's kicks where one can, however sad they may be!).

2   **Make lists.** What seems like a mountain of work often looks far less daunting when you get it into a list of actions on a single sheet of paper. Don't try to carry it all around with you in your head. Take great pleasure in ticking things off on your lists. To give yourself a good start, always jot something on to your list that you have already done, and tick it off straight away.

3   **Don't take lots of work home.** Try to finish what you can at school. Take one thing home and get it done. Otherwise you end up lugging a heavy bag home every night and not achieving what you hoped. We think it is better to try to do less, but to get it done.

4   **Don't do it unless it is worth it.** 'How will it help pupils learn?' has to be the question you use to judge what it is worth investing your time and energy in.

5   **Make space for your own development.** If you don't want to be an IT coordinator for the whole of your career (or even if you do), develop some skills and strengths for yourself, too. More cynically, remember Higgins' Law of Promotion, 'she who innovates, escalates'. If you want to get on, get involved in a new initiative. This can look great on paper when all you had to do was show up to a couple of steering group meetings!

6   **Use administrative and support staff.** You do not have to do it all alone. There are may time consuming tasks which can reasonably be passed on to others. Teachers are not good at asking others to do things for them. Surprising though it may seem, administration and support staff are often much *better* at doing administration and support than are teachers!

7   **Keep learning.** In the world of ICT there is continual, incessant innovation. The educational scene has not been without its changes in the recent past, so it is difficult to keep your own agenda. But remember that the more you learn, the more you want to learn. Experience is not the same as learning. You acquire experience regardless, but not everyone learns from it.

8   **Don't worry about it.** There is a limit to what you can achieve, and it is not worth getting stressed because you can't get everything done. Far better to be ready for the day ahead than to deprive yourself of a much needed rest because your scheme of work is up for review in a month's time and you still have X, Y and Z to do before then.

9   **Have some fun.** Make sure you have some space to enjoy yourself. That means *not* at the computer. Really – no matter how exciting the latest game is, or the thread of the e-mail discussion group. Talk to people, not about your job either!

10 **Remember why you came into teaching.** Focus on the parts of the job you enjoy, this is likely to be teaching the pupils! Organizing your time so you can enjoy this more will help get you through the bits that aren't quite so good.

11 **Get a life.** Friends and family still need you, and you need them. Indulge them from time to time. Use whatever means you can to keep a sense of perspective on your work. You must keep time for yourself and your friends and family.

Chapter 10   The Internet

We have repeatedly suggested that in the world of ICT, everything changes, and that this happens so quickly it is almost impossible to keep up with it. But there are one or two certainties, and one is that the Internet is here to stay. This is the principal form of high speed, accessible, global communication and will be with us for long enough to make investing time and effort in getting connected, training staff and integrating digital sources of information into classroom practice worth while.

The visionaries will tell you that we are on the edge of perhaps the greatest advance in educational thinking since the introduction of compulsory education for all. This may be true, but it can be difficult to see that far when the reality is that many teachers are struggling to get to grips with how best to use their trusty BBC Master with 35, all too enthusiastic five-year-olds!

This chapter is an introduction to what the Internet is, a guide on how to explore it and a few suggestions about how to use it in the context of primary teaching. We also offer suggestions of e-mail, which can be a vital means of communication across the planet, but can also be an excellent way of communicating with colleagues and pupils on a one-to-one basis.

53

What is the Internet?

In a brief break from the regular format of this book, this section is not offered as a series of tips, but as an overview for the uninitiated of what the Internet actually is! We trust that colleagues who already know this will press on and not be insulted by our attempt here to start from scratch.

The Internet is basically a global network of computers, connected by various forms of telephone line (various as in ordinary telephone cables, higher speed ISDN phone lines, very high speed optical cable and slightly more mind-boggling technologies such as satellite and microwave!). But more importantly, it is also a way of communicating and cooperating with people from all over the globe. This communicating and cooperating can take a few different forms as outlined below.

E-mail. E-mail is a relatively simple form of communication and very easy to get to grips with. Everyone who has an e-mail account (usually given free with any Internet connection) has an e-mail address and, therefore, can send and receive e-mail. E-mail works in principally the same way as conventional mail. You write a message, address it to the person who you want to send it to, and then tell your computer to send it! Precisely how it gets there can remain a mystery to all but the most ardent anoraks; all that is important is that it is quick, easy and amazingly reliable! It is also very inexpensive. It is also quite addictive!

Video conferencing. Video conferencing is a rather more complex form of communication via the Internet (or between a networked series of computers or terminals called an Intranet). It involves a few pieces of extra kit and additional software, but principally allows two people or small groups, who are connected to the Internet, to link up in a one-to-one or one-to a few situation and 'talk' to one another in what techies call 'real time'. Currently the verb 'talk' has to be used loosely, as 'talk' can really mean 'type' unless you both have a very high speed link to the Internet. Even with supposedly high speed ISDN lines, talking is far from a reliable method of communicating. But its advantage over e-mail is that, as long as all parties have access to a digitizing camera, you can actually see the person you are talking to! More simply, 'computer conferencing' is about using the Internet (or an Intranet) just to send text messages as replies or starter-pages to a 'conference' that can be read simultaneously by many readers.

The World Wide Web. This is the bit that has all the web pages and sites that you hear so much about. Basically, anyone with an Internet connection can have a web site. People and institutions that have web sites publish, and make available, information pages and downloadable software that contain information about almost anything and everything for anyone to get at. To help you find what you want, various companies have set up vast databases of web sites. These are called search engines. WWW information is viewed by a piece of software called a browser.

Telnet. Telnet is a system by which you can connect to someone else's computer over a phone line. It tends to be for services such as weather watching or checking library catalogues, rapidly becoming an ancient geek dialect.

54

Why get connected?

There are any number of reasons to get yourself connected to the Internet – some good and some bad. It is fairly important that any school gets connected for the right reasons, and that it knows what those reasons are. Start with the previous section (just so that you know the difference between different services), then consider why you want to get connected. You may find it useful to consider the following possible reasons, and work out which of these are most important to you, your pupils and your school.

1   **Because you have to.** Whether you like it or not, the government wants every school, every public sector institution come to that, to be connected to the Internet by the year 2002.

2   **Because there is a lot of information out there.** The Word Wide Web is the largest body of information ever assembled. It would be a shame not to give your school, and the children in it, access to this, especially when you consider that it costs relatively little if used wisely.

3   **Because there is no point swimming against the tide.** At least there is no point swimming against the tide for too long! The Internet and all the tools it provides are potentially very useful to education. The current situation may well be that teachers have to put in quite a bit of leg work (or is it finger work?) to get the best out of it, but things are changing quickly.

4   **Because children and teachers are going to have to deal with increasing amounts of information.** It is going to become a way of working that every child will need to have some experience of, and that every teacher will have to learn to deal with it.

5   **Because learning how to organize and structure information is essential.**
Children will need experience of putting information into the system, as
well as taking it out. The Internet provides a huge range of *real* audiences
for children to learn how to make contact with, and to communicate with
efficiently and accurately.

6   **Because e-mail is so easy.** Even if e-mail is the only Internet service you
deal with, it may well be worth it because it is so quick, so easy and so
reliable (although that is not to say that the recipient will be!).

7   **Because video conferencing is so motivating.** Communicating with
people from all over the globe is one thing, but being able to see them
while you talk to them is really exciting, even the children quite like it!
But imagine being able to connect to a NASA scientist and have your
class ask them questions, and to get them to demonstrate as well as to
explain their answers. You may think that this is taking community links
a little far – but what an opportunity!

8   **Because it offers a wealth of other opportunities.** Sharing and exchanging
ideas and information across continents, cultures, faiths and huge
distances means that Internet services actually make the National
Curriculum for geography, for instance, a little more realistic!

9   **Because it will help to prepare your children for the 'real' world.**
Whatever that might be! It may be a little terrifying, but access to and use
of the Internet is rapidly establishing itself as a 'life skill' and the majority
of your pupils need to acquire it! The Internet will surely evolve, but it
will endure.

10 **Because it just might help you to teach, too.** Given the time to find out,
you may find that access to the Internet helps you to do your job better!
You can find new stuff more quickly (although some of it may be of a
poor standard at the moment), and it may become the most powerful
teaching and learning tool you have, and with relatively little preparation.
This may all sound like Internet evangelism but, believe us, this is really
mild by comparison to what the powers that be will tell you!

55

Getting connected

Many people will tell you scary stories about trying to get themselves or their schools connected to the Internet. They can't all be wrong! It isn't as straightforward as it probably should be, but it is getting a lot better. The following tips are based on our personal experiences of getting on-line.

1   **Be prepared.** Before you start the process of even telephoning an Internet Service Provider (ISP: who will effectively sell you a connection to the Internet, an e-mail account and so on), make sure you have a suitable modem, a newish computer with at least 16 MB of real memory, a convenient phone line socket, a CD-ROM player (not absolutely essential), some paper, a pencil, a headache remedy and about two days of free time. Make sure everything is connected (except the paper and pencil) according to the instructions in the manual. You may also have to configure one or two pieces of software, but this should be explained in the handbook, too! It is getting easier, and with modern equipment you may simply have to insert the CD-ROM and follow on-screen instructions for an hour or two!

2   **Don't do it alone.** If possible, try to get someone who has done it at least once before, on the same sort of machine for preference, to help in person, or to sit at the other end of a telephone and offer moral support. Perhaps you can persuade a technician from the IT centre or the local comprehensive school to talk you through it.

3   **Don't listen to the first person who gives you advice.** Beware especially if they are telling you how easy it is! The more you talk about it, the more sense the process will begin to make and if it begins to make a little sense, then that's a good start.

4   **Choose an ISP.** Getting the right ISP is a bit of a hit or a miss affair. If a friend or colleague has one they think is good, that would be a good place to start. If the connection is for school, you may want to get a 'filtered' service that, in theory, blocks undesirable sites. Research Machines'

'Internet for Learning' service is an example. Really, these are 'content providers' rather than ISPs, but the principle is similar.

5   **Check the service levels of your chosen ISP.** Things to watch out for are details such as how many e-mail accounts they will provide for free (the more the merrier), whether they give you free web space so that your school can publish its own web site (the bigger the better), whether they will offer to sell you additional space if you need it and how much it is (compare prices). Also check whether there are any access restrictions, perhaps the times of day that access to their servers is available; most are 24 hours, but it is worth checking.

6   **Have two or three possible 'user names' prepared.** You will be asked to give a user name when you ring your chosen ISP. This will be the name that they recognize you by; it will become part of your e-mail and your web site address and it should have something to do with your school. So, Hangem High School might choose 'Hangem' or 'HangemHigh' or 'HangemSchool' as possible user names. It is important to have more than one possibility because your name has to be unique, and if your first choice is already taken by someone somewhere else in the world, you'll need one in reserve.

7   **Have a couple of passwords prepared.** Your ISP may give you a password when you call, or they may ask you for one. Try to pick something you will remember easily, such as the schools' post code or the name of your cat! It will need to be kept a secret as it is the only thing that prevents others from getting access to your ISP, your e-mail, and so on. Other people who know your password could run up huge phone bills in your name, or maybe even order goods that will land on your desk!

8   **With all your kit prepared, ring the ISP.** Almost all run a 24-hour service and, if you are confident enough to try, most will also give you a URL (see Internet abbreviations) where you can get the relevant software to automate much of the process. If you would rather not try this, they will probably mail you a disk-based version of the software instead. They may well offer software such as browsers and e-mail applications, too. Take them up on it – it can't hurt!

9   **Write everything clearly and exactly.** You need to make sure that everything the operator tells you is copied down exactly, capitals in the right places, spaces exactly where you are told! Be particularly careful with punctuation, full stops, slashes, and so on. Double-check everything you write down. One tiny mistake can put you back about a week's worth of spare time!

10 **Wait for the software.** If you are not confident about trying to download software, wait for the disks to arrive. It should only take a couple of days.

11 **Install the software.** If there are any 'help' or 'readme' files, print them out and scan through them to get an idea of what they say.

12 **Follow guidelines step by step.** Read carefully, if you are not sure what a particular step means, ring the ISP help line back. Don't forget you can't connect if you are on a phone using the same line to talk to your ISP as your computer is using to connect it to the server!

13 **Cross your fingers and give it a go.** It isn't impossible to get it right first time but…

14 **If it doesn't work first time, don't be surprised.** Just ring your ISP and get them to talk you through it again, they are usually very helpful. Borrowing a mobile phone to do this may sound expensive, but may stop you tearing your hair out, or trying to enter your configuration settings with an axe.

15 **If it does work first time, buy a lottery ticket.** It is clearly your lucky day!

16 **Don't be put off by all this gloom and doom.** It can be tricky the first time, but isn't everything? We have tried to be honest about how it feels, if only to convince you that, when you don't succeed first time, you're in good company!

56

Getting going with e-mail

E-mail is perhaps the easiest and the most useful aspect of the Internet. It is certainly a good place to start for any novice, and the really nice thing about it is that it works in a perfectly real and understandable way. It's just like ordinary mail only quicker (much quicker) and cheaper (much cheaper) and fun (much more fun)…

1   **Use it yourself first.** There is little point trying to use it with your class until you have used it a few times yourself, and feel confident that it works, and that you know how to make it work.

2   **Start small.** Everyone must know someone with an e-mail address. Get in touch with them via a system that you know works, such as the telephone and let them know you want to try out your e-mail. Copy their address very carefully and go step by step through the help sheet (that you will have printed out). You don't need to be connected at this point, only connect when you have finished the message and want to send it. Get them to send you a reply, you'll be amazed how quickly you hear back.

3   **Notice how easy it is to 'reply'.** You don't normally have to key in an e-mail address when you reply to an incoming message, you just select 'reply' from a menu, and the software gives you a screen on which you can enter the text of your reply. When you send your reply, the software will add your own username and e-mail address automatically – more things to think about less.

4   **Look for someone to talk to.** You can try just writing to an organization whose e-mail address you just happen to have come across, but it is much better to have a specific person or group to write to. If you know who your audience is, it is much easier to know what to say to them. Try looking on bulletin boards, search for schools with web sites or ask your local ICT centre for help.

5   **Remember that you get out what you put in**. If you send a lot of e-mails, you'll get a lot of e-mails. Some of them may be useless, but most of them won't!

6   **Work off-line.** E-mail applications do not require you to have an open connection to the Internet to be used You only need to connect when you are actually ready to send them, and even then many will connect themselves automatically. You can get the class to write e-mails all day long and then connect up yourself at the end of the day and send them all off at once!

7   **Be careful with attachments.** It is possible to send all sorts of different files via e-mail. Files such as pictures, stories, even multimedia presentations can be attached to an e-mail and downloaded so that the recipient can get hold of them and use them on their machines. There are two things to watch out for. Firstly, files need to be compressed (just to save time and money as smaller files get transferred quickly), you will need an additional, free program that will 'stuff' (on Apple Mac) or 'Zip' (on windows machines) your file for you. The other is to make sure that the person at the other end can unstuff or unzip the file, and that they have the appropriate applications to be able to view the files you sent. You'll soon find out who can read your attachments, and whose you can read.

8   **Don't attach text only files.** (Unless they have a specific format that must be maintained.) It is quicker and easier to copy text from a text file and paste it into the e-mail, rather than attaching the file. E-mail is already as compressed as possible.

9   **Try to build up a dialogue.** It is really easy to get a dialogue going between two classes, two small groups or just two individuals using e-mail. This is very motivating, provides an audience for children's writing and gets them using ICT constructively.

10 **Try to give the children open access.** Once your class are familiar with the use of e-mail they may be able to use it on a 'real life' basis. If parents, for example, have e-mail at work or at home, possibilities include, 'Dad, forgot packed lunch, can you bring it to school please?' or, 'Mum, football practice is cancelled, can you pick me up at…', and so on.

11 **Draw up a few rules for the use of e-mail.** These could be agreed with the whole class and could include things such as, 'I won't read anyone else's e-mail without permission' or, 'I will tell the teacher if there is anything in an e-mail that I think should not be there' or, 'I will only connect to the Internet when the teacher is in the class', and so on.

57

Using the World Wide Web

Many schools and teachers will be concerned with providing decent access to the World Wide Web. They will want to make sure that the time they spend on-line is used efficiently and that children are protected from undesirable material. Here are some suggestions for making good use of the web.

Access for teachers:

1   **If you get the bug, get connected at home.** There is so much out there and so little free time available in school, the only way many teachers can find the time to track down what they need is if they have an Internet connection to their home. Some ISPs, which specialize in services for education, offer teachers a discounted rate if their schools are already connected through them.

2   **Get hold of bookmarks from others.** Other teachers in other schools and the IT centre may well be happy to swap 'bookmarks' with you. Bookmarks are links to sites you find useful and getting hold of someone else's means you don't have to do so much searching. See Appendix 3 for some places to start.

3   **Set up your own home page.** If you are feeling ambitious, try making your own home page, the first page you see when you open your browser. This can contain links to all the sites that you use on a regular basis, and while you will never be able to do without the facility to search for new sites, less experienced users will be able to get at what they want quickly, and you will know that it is relatively safe.

4   **Look for educational and teacher-specific services.** Some companies such as Research Machines, BT, the BBC and ICL are heavily involved in promoting educational use of the WWW. If you use these services, you know that what they offer is far more likely to be relevant.

5   **Share what you find.** Sharing is what the WWW is really all about and teachers, possibly more than anyone, need to share their experiences of using it. We are our one source of relatively unbiased advice! Look out for bulletin boards run by your LEA or others committed to education (maybe even the Government, at a push!).

For children:

1   **Consider where Internet machines should be sited.** They need to be accessible to all the children that you want to benefit, but they also need to be sited where they can be supervised effectively. In one classroom is no good, but in the library it may be too difficult to supervise adequately!

2   **Bookmark.** Especially in the early stages as it is important to ensure children's success, and one way is to bookmark sites you want them to visit.

3   **Look out for education-specific sites or ones that are clearly child-oriented.** Bookmark these and steer the children towards them when you get the chance. There are child-centred search engines, too, such as Yahooligans, that only offer suitable links.

4   **Consider whether they could design their own home page.** It may sound like a tall order, but it isn't really as hard as you might think. It is actually a good task on presenting information.

5   **Look out for free filters.** Filters are pieces of software that block sites that contain certain words in their home pages or descriptions. The list is user configurable, so you can put in the words that you want to block. They are not perfect, but they are a good weapon in the arsenal! Look out for the likes of NetNanny and WebGuardian.

6   **Make sure that there is no access without teacher supervision.** This will probably have to be a rule that you expect children to stick to.

7   **Do spot checks on history or cache files.** Histories or cache files work automatically and a brief check, every now and then, will let you know whether the sites that are being visited are appropriate and relevant. Let the children know you can do this, too – it may act as a good deterrent to inappropriate use.

8　**Establish rules of Netiquette.** Netiquette can be a series of guidelines that users agree to abide by. They could include things such as, 'I won't enter a site that says I am too young to look at it' or, 'If I come across a site that contains things I think I probably shouldn't see, I will close the window and tell the teacher' or, 'The Internet is for everyone, everyone has the right to use it', and so on.

58

Publishing on the web

Actually, publishing things on the WWW, either on your own web site or on other, public access forums, is getting quite sophisticated. But, as is so often the case, it is not as hard as you might think and children pick up the idea pretty quickly, especially if you have done some multimedia work with them before. Clearly, you aren't going to want to rush in to web publishing with children in Key Stage 1, but older pupils, if introduced to it in the right way, can produce good results quite quickly. Here are some ways of getting them started.

1   **Gather samples first.** The best place to start is by looking at sites produced by people in similar situations as you. It will give you an idea of what is possible, but also some inspiration for your own ideas.

2   **Have a go yourself.** As stated, it isn't as hard as you might think, because modern software does all the programming for you. Not long ago, writing in HTML (HyperText Markup Language) was a matter of typing in line upon line of HTML code; now authoring software does all the HTML and DHTML (Dynamic HyperText Markup Language) work in the background while you just get on with typing in what you want, where you want it on each web page.

3   **Look at good and bad samples with the children.** While the good samples will give you ideas, the bad ones will give you ideas of what to try to avoid. Try to decide between you what it is that makes some sites bad. Are they slow to download? Do they lack links and things to click? Are there too many pictures and not enough information?

4   **Start small.** A good place to start is with a single page, probably a home page that you don't actually upload to your server, but keep on the hard disk of your computer. Once it is written, you tell your browser to open this page every time it is launched and then your class page, with all your favourite links on, is your launch pad to the WWW.

5 **Stick with what you already know.** If you have done a little desktop publishing, it might be that your desktop publishing software can save files in HTML code. If it can, you will find it very easy to do your first page. If not, you will still be able to copy and paste bits of text and even graphics and charts from your DTP package into your web authoring package (such as 'HomePage' or 'PageMill').

6 **Make sure you buy appropriate software.** If you are going to purchase specific web authoring software, make sure it is WYSIWYG (What You See Is What You Get), so that you don't have to get involved in writing HTML code. Software such as 'Web Workshop' is WYSIWYG *and* child-oriented and might be a good place to start. (The only drawback is that it encourages children to incorporate a lot of graphics, which lead to very long download times.)

7 **Once your confidence grows, go for a whole site!** If you have tried and succeeded in putting together a single home page, then try to add a few pages to it. Adapt the original page to give links to one or two new projects. You will probably need to consider uploading at this point – ring your ISP help line for advice.

8 **Try to keep your site low maintenance**. If you include lots of detailed information about the school football team it will be out of date within a week unless someone takes on the role of maintaining it week in and week out. Try to go for stuff that only changes more slowly.

9 **Nothing motivates like feedback.** If you include a page about jokes, or poetry, invite people who visit your site to respond, or send you new ideas. Include your e-mail address and watch your children's faces as they read their first feedback e-mail!

10 **Be prepared to use and be used**. The web is all about sharing. Don't be too surprised if others take your ideas and your pictures to use for themselves, that is what is so good about the web. They will do it to you, and you should do it to them!

59

Off-line use

Many Internet services can be used off-line, without actually being linked up to the net. There are many significant benefits to doing this if you can. Here are some suggestions about getting the most from the Internet while off-line.

1   **Do as much as possible off-line.** It is quicker and cheaper if you work as much as possible without being connected. The WWW has not been dubbed the 'World Wide Wait' for nothing and the more you wait while connected, the more it costs. Also, the more people there are needlessly connected, the slower the situation becomes.

2   **Always read and write e-mails off-line.** Everything you could want to do in an e-mail can be done off-line, except actually sending them, and even that can be done automatically. It may take minutes or even hours to compose an e-mail or to read a cluster of incoming ones, but it only takes a few seconds to send and receive them. You only need pay for the few seconds' connection time.

3   **Download useful pages.** Most browsers allow you to download pages of useful information, storing them on your own computer so that you can look at them in more detail later without a live connection. Remember to clear out things you've finished with, to make sure your computer does not get its hard disk full.

4   **Get software to help with downloads.** Pieces of software, such as (TT) 'WebBuddy' or 'WebWhacker', can actually download linked pages or whole sites so that the whole thing can be used off-line.

5   **Grab useful images as you browse.** While not strictly off-line use, try to get into the habit of collecting images you think might be useful later. On an Apple Mac, just click and hold on the image you want. On PC, hold down the right button in the image you want and follow instructions.

This means that you can do further detailed work on the images later, when you're off-line, and you don't have to waste on-line time going back looking for where you first noticed the interesting images.

6   **Don't surf.** Perhaps the biggest waste of time! You may want to surf, in private, the first few times you go on the web, just to get a feel for what is out there. But when working in the classroom always plan what you are looking for and where you think you might find it away from the computer to minimize time spent actually on-line.

7   **Use CD-ROM encyclopaedias to develop searching skills.** To get pupils used to the way a search engine works, identifying useful key words and so on, use a CD-ROM-based research program for a few weeks leading up to the maiden voyage! The skills used are highly transferable.

8   **Look out for browser-based manuals and help sheets.** More software is being supplied with help manuals written in HTML, which is viewable and searchable by an ordinary browser. These are quite good for developing searching and navigational skills without being connected.

9   **If you are feeling ambitious, why not go the whole hog?** The whole hog being setting up your own Intranet, an in-house version of the Internet. It works by downloading whole web sites onto a computer in the school (see tip 4), and then that computer acts as a server to every other computer that is equipped to have network connections and can handle a web browser. This is not for the faint-hearted, and we would not recommend you try this by yourself unless you have some experience of networking, networking protocols and a good chunk of free time! It is cheaper, safer and more reliable (eventually), but it is a major project for even experienced users.

10 **If you do set up an Intranet, make the most of it.** You could then use the best and fastest machine to do the on-line browsing and downloading from the web, and use older or slower machines for Intranet access, which costs nothing once set up. An Intranet is also excellent for in-school e-mail communications, and for allowing pupils on a number of machines to enter e-mails to be sent out via the web from time to time when the main machine is put on-line.

60

Browser tips

Your browser is your window on to the Internet, and as browsers (eg, 'Netscape' and 'Internet Explorer') get more and more sophisticated, they also help you to do what you need to on the web faster, more efficiently and more reliably. Here are some tips for finding out about your browser.

1   **Watch what happens to the pointer.** As you move your pointer over different parts of a web page, watch what happens to it. If it turns into a finger, you have just gone over a clickable hot spot. If it turns into a text insertion point (like a capital I) you can insert text, and so on.

2   **Watch what happens to clicked links.** Links on a web page tend to be different colours or highlighted with a blue line. This is to help you identify links more easily. When you have clicked on a link, it usually changes colour so you can avoid going down the same blind alley twice!

3   **You can use your browser to grab information from the web.** You can usually highlight text and copy it, or click and grab images from web pages relatively easily.

4   **Use the Back button.** When you have followed a link that turns out to be a waste of time, clicking on Back takes you a step back the way you came. You can usually click back any number of times, but it can be slow as you wait for links to be made so…

5   **Open the windows.** Browsers allow you to 'open new windows'. This actually means that you can have a stack of web sites open all at the same time, piled up on top of one another, each in a different window. This can be very useful when following a link you are unsure about, if you open that new link in a new window and it turns out to be a red herring, just close the window and you are back to where you started from.

6   **Use Bookmarks (or 'Favourites' in Microsoft Internet Explorer).**
    Bookmarks are a way of recording and recalling URLs (Universal Resource
    Locators: this is the term for the addresses of web pages) to useful sites
    and save a great deal of time. In your browser, go to the menu marked
    'Bookmarks' or 'Favourites', click and hold and then go down to
    'Bookmark Page' or 'Add page to Favourites'. When you want them again,
    go back to the same menu, click and hold and then go down to the relevant
    bookmark.

7   **Find out what the buttons in the toolbar do.** They are there for a purpose,
    and are configurable, too. For instance, the 'Search' button takes you to a
    search engine, you can select any search engine you like. 'Stop' makes the
    page that is in the process of being downloaded stop, so you can get on
    with something else, and so on.

8   **Don't pursue every prompt for a plug-in.** Sometimes, as a page
    downloads you will get a message saying that your browser does not
    have the appropriate plug-in. Plug-ins are additional pieces of software
    that add extra capabilities to your browser, but downloading can take
    quite a while and it could be for a plug-in that you will never use again.
    Go for ones that turn up a lot, but leave the rest.

9   **Try altering window sizes and screen resolutions.** Web pages are funny
    things in that, unlike printed pages, they do not have a set length or width.
    If you are getting a cropped image or everything looks a bit misshapen,
    try altering the size of your browser's window. Sometimes trying higher,
    or lower screen resolutions helps, too. (Look for screen controls in 'Control'
    menus.)

10 **Look out for Drag 'n' Drop.** Drag and drop is a way of transferring text
    or images from one application to another without having to copy and
    paste. It usually just involves clicking and holding on the resource you
    want and dragging it to the place where you want it to be. Not all browsers
    and not all applications let you do this, but if they do, they can save you
    lots of time.

61

Searching the web

It is perfectly possible to wile away an hour of two (or even a week or two) getting absolutely nowhere on the web. Performing effective searches is something you may need to learn for yourself, as well as teach the children, to make sure you get to where you want to be as quickly as possible. Here are some tips on making searches productive.

1   **Click in the space or box next to the 'Search' button to enter keywords.**
    If you have managed to find a search engine, you will need to click in the small white space next to the button marked 'Search'. Don't worry about the size of the box though, you can enter as many words as you need.

2   **Cultivate a search engine that suits you.** To find anything on the WWW, if you don't know its URL (web address) already, you will need to use a search engine. These are basically huge, automated databases that you can use to search for keywords, topics, and so on. If you find one that makes sense to you, stick with it, the chances are that as you delve deeper, it will reveal a great many new ways of working effectively.

3   **Start with index-based searches.** Index-based searches, such as 'Yahoo', are a way of moving from broad topics to more specific topics; so if you are searching for something about the Spanish Armada you might start from a broad topic such as 'History'. This will give you a series of headings from which you might choose 'European', which will give a series of headings from which you might choose 'Famous Battles', and so on.

4   **Other forms of search can also be useful, however.** Searching via keywords can be useful, but the matches tend to be very random. Data about sites is often collected automatically, so matching three words in a site's home page, say 'education', 'history' and 'Spain', could give you matches for everything from the history of Spanish education to 101 traditional Spanish recipes!

5   **If you are going to use key word searches – start big!** Try to use as many
     keywords as possible at first because it is easy to get a message such as
     'Matches 1–20 out of 1 726 432 possible matches for search: 'famous,
     Spanish, battles'. The computer would then display the first 20, and
     continue for hours if you went on, until you've seen all 1 726 432! The
     more keywords you use, the more likely you are to get decent matches.

6   **Don't just play.** Even in the early stages of using the web you will learn
     more if you search for something specific, than if you just try something
     to see where you end up.

7   **Don't follow anything that looks like an advert.** Banners and adverts
     offering all the riches of the orient will probably take you somewhere
     totally useless. If that is where you want to go, fine, but some adverts are
     a little more subtle and try to lead you to sites by offering you a more
     intellectual reason to try it. If a link looks a little out of context with the
     rest of the page, it's probably best avoided.

8   **Before visiting a site mentioned in the results of a search, check its
     URL.** The URL is that string of gobbledegook with lots of slashes and
     dots. The last part of the URL gives some indication of the sort of
     establishment running the site. For instance: if it ends in '.edu' it will be
     an American educational establishment; if '.ac' it may be a British (or
     Australian/New Zealand, or others) university or college; if '.com' it will
     probably be a commercial company; if '.org' it will probably be a non-
     profit or governmental institution; and '.uk' indicates a British site.

9   **Practice makes perfect.** There are no really good, quick fixes when
     searching for sites. The best way is a little practice on a regular basis and
     try to become an expert in one way of working, rather than a jack-of-all-
     trades. There are always a hundred routes to the same place, it's just a
     question of finding the sort of route that suits you best.

10   **If you feel like you are wasting too much time, try an advanced search.**
     Advanced searches are supposed to help you to search more efficiently,
     but only if you know what you want. When you feel confident enough,
     give them a go.

62

Internet abbreviations

Nothing generates bizarre abbreviations like the world of ICT. Even when you know what an abbreviation stands for, it doesn't necessarily mean you will understand what it is for or what it does! Here are short explanations of a few of the more common ones. In practice, you don't need to know what they mean, you just need to know what to do with them!

@   Actually means 'at' and is usually part of an e-mail address. It sits between the user name and the domain name, the user being the person who receives the mail and the domain being the part of the server that is dedicated to that person.

FTP   Stands for File Transfer Protocol and is just a way of transferring files from one machine connected to the Internet to another. When you upload or download software or web pages you will probably use an application that uses FTP.

HTML   Stands for HyperText Markup Language. This is the programming code that is used to put web pages together. Few less than professional users need to know much more about it than that. It is in the process of being superseded by DHTML, or Dynamic HyperText Markup Language, which offers greater flexibility.

HTTP   Stands for HyperText Transfer Protocol and is the process by which HTML is transferred from one Internet computer to another. You will see it at the beginning of most web site addresses.

IP   Stands for Internet Protocol and any computer linked to the Internet needs an IP number. This number ensures that pieces of information that are sent across the Internet get to where they were going.

TCP   Transfer Communications Protocol, a sort of Esperanto for computers that lets them establish communications. You may need the antiseptic version after you damage yourself and the computer when it refuses to communicate via any transfer protocol.

URL   Stands for Universal Resource Locator but is actually a fancy name for a web sites address. (We acknowledge the cries of derision from the world's anoraks.) An URL is that weird string of letters and symbols that goes something like (http://www.wonderful.brilliant.co/index.html) – there is no full stop right at the end. You should be able to identify various parts of this URL from this list of abbreviations.

WWW   Stands for the World Wide Web, or the 'World Wide Wait!' and is often further abbreviated to W3.

Chapter 11 Troubleshooting, Top Good Habits and Home–school Links

In this final short chapter, we offer just a few brief sections that are our best ideas for some areas not covered in the preceding chapters. These are about solving common technical problems, and some suggestions for teaching in the classroom and developing links with children's experience at home.

63

If it doesn't work...

The most efficient way of troubleshooting is to promote awareness and understanding among all staff and pupils. If they are aware of what can go wrong, and have a few ideas about how to put it right, then one of the major stumbling blocks for the implementation of ICT in schools can be reduced – a little – hopefully! Try copying these suggestions, and offer them to each member of staff before calling out the emergency services! If it doesn't work...

1   **Is it plugged in?** And don't just check the electrical sockets, check that you know where the mouse, keyboard, monitor, disk drive and printer should be plugged in and then make sure they are. Make sure they are all switched on, too.

2   **Look for a light to see if power is getting through.** If there is no power light on, could the electrical connection have failed, it may just need a new fuse!

3   **Check all fuses.** There may be a number of fuses in any electrical chain, one in the plug, one in the extension socket, one in each of the plugs that go into that, any or many could have failed.

4   **Are the brightness and contrast buttons turned up?** Check because we have all fallen for this one at one time or another. One of us remembers spending a very sad day thinking he had broken his new computer, not realizing he had knocked the brightness control right down!

5   **Check the leads.** Are they damaged in any way?

6   **Look for option switches.** Things that could inadvertently have been set incorrectly, everything from the 40/80 track switch on an old BBC to the SCSI ID switch on a CD drive.

7   **What has changed since last time?** If it worked before, something must have been altered since last time. If you can work out what, you will have solved your problem.

8   **How did you fix it last time?** If you have seen the problem before, do what you did last time (as long as it worked).

9   **Are the batteries fully charged?** If there is a spare set, try them to see if you get any joy.

10 **Is it correctly formatted?** It may be that the floppy disk you are about to use is not compatible with the machine you are trying to use it in!

11 **Is it locked?** Files and applications can be electronically locked to stop them from being tampered with. Check to see if any protection is installed on your computer.

12 **Is it full?** If the disk is full, either throw something away or get a new disk.

13 **Does it have enough memory?** It is easy to leave applications running on more modern computers and these can take up large amounts of memory. This may cause a memory shortage, which can cause all sorts of weird problems, so quit anything that is not actually being used.

14 **Do you have the right driver?** Many peripheral devices require special bits of software to make them work. Is the software you have the right sort?

15 **Is it going already?** You might have launched an application already and that's why its icon looks strange and it doesn't seem to do what it normally does!

16 **Is a button jammed down?** A button on the keyboard or a volume control that is stuck in can cause all sorts of problems. Unstick them and try to clean them with an appropriate cleaner.

17 **Can you make it happen again?** Sometimes problems are just one-offs. If you can't repeat the problem, it is probably safe to ignore it!

18 **Are you running a new piece of software that might have caused a conflict?** If you are, try removing it and starting again.

19   **Try to remember to run diagnostic software, if you have it.** Every time your computer hangs or crashes you are supposed to run some sort of fault diagnosis software. In reality, few people have the time, but try to do it once in a while as a precautionary measure.

20   **Keep a record of error messages.** You may not know what they mean, but someone, somewhere might.

21   **Use the fault sheet before asking for help.** (For obvious reasons!)

64

The top 12 good habits to teach...

These are the sorts of things that staff and pupils need to get into the habit of doing, it will save them and you a lot of grief in the long run!

1 **Save before you print!** The number of times things go wrong at the moment when you try to print is incredible. If you save your file *before* printing, you won't lose it, and you could also save yourself a lot of additional work!

2 **Check spelling before you print.** There is nothing worse than wasted ink when running a spell checker could so easily have corrected errors first!

3 **Give files sensible names.** Calling your file 'hello' or 'myName' or 'new' or 'today' isn't likely to give you much of a clue what it is or what it's about. It will not help anyone else to work out what to do with it either!

4 **Save it in the proper place.** If you have set up a folder or area of the disk for work to be saved in, put it there, it will make finding it later so much easier!

5 **If you can't find it later, try 'Find File' or 'Browse'.** Both functions let you search for missing files, as long as you know roughly what its name is or when it was created.

6 **Print once.** And if it doesn't work, don't just print again, try to find out why it didn't work the first time. Many an additional copy has mysteriously appeared out of the printer when the real problem has been cured! Phil's 1st Law of printing states that, 'A printer *knows* when something is really urgent, and likes to establish its control over you by choosing such times to run out of ink, jam paper, and decide that you really wanted to print landscape rather than portrait'.

7   **Type first, present later.** Messing around with layout, sizes and fonts before work is completed is just an excuse not to think about what you are supposed to be doing.

8   **The space bar is not for spacing!** Well actually it is, but if you want to put a bit of text in the centre of the page or indent paragraphs, the tab button or the alignment buttons are much better. (If you use the space bar, when you change font sizes, the spaces change too so you're back to square one!)

9   **Don't forget to exit or quit!** This is not the same as *closing* a window. Closing leaves the application still running in the background, where it takes up memory and could cause problems.

10   **Read – and think about – error messages *before* clicking 'OK'.** Firstly, if you don't you might lose all your work. Secondly, it will probably help whoever has to fix it if they know what the computer's final words were before passing away.

11   **Hitting it harder won't make it work any faster *or* better!** Like as not it will have the reverse effect. It may make you feel good in the short term, but do try not to!

12   **And finally, one for the pupils: 'Don't do as the teacher does, do as the teacher says!'** And we all know why, don't we?

65

Developing home–school links

Schools need to keep parents up to date with what is going on at school, and ICT is one area which most parents now expect schools to be working on. There are a variety of ways home–school links can be developed. Here are some ideas to start with.

1   **Tell home about what you are doing in school.** This might be on a notice board, in a letter, with an exhibition, through the local press, a web page, in the annual report or any of the many ways schools communicate with parents and carers.

2   **Include pupils' ICT work in newsletters.** Why not get children to design a cover or section, or get them to produce the programme for the summer performance? It may take longer, but it is a really practical and public way to get children's work seen.

3   **Focus on the learning benefits.** Some parents and carers may be sceptical of the benefits of using ICT, particularly with young children. If you can show them examples of how ICT helps children to learn, they will be easier to convince.

4   **Suggest activities for children to do at home.** Children who use computers at home tend to make more progress with IT at school. A leaflet or parents' workshop, with some ideas for home use, will be welcomed. You may even want to recommend some software for different types of computers.

5   **Develop a progression of home activities.** If you start with one year-group you could extend your leaflet into a booklet over the next couple of years.

6   **Show them what pupils do at school.** Most parents will not have seen programmable robots or control technology. Organizing a session for them will help them to see the educational benefits, and may recruit you a few classroom volunteers, too.

7   **Have an ICT exhibition.** This will not only get parents in, particularly if you have children demonstrating, but will also emphasize the importance of ICT at school.

8   **Reassure them about the Internet.** Many parents have anxieties about the sort of material that is available on the web. A letter, or better still an open evening demonstrating how the Internet will be used and the safeguards you have in place, will help to put their minds at ease.

9   **Find out what children do at home with computers.** Asking them and their parents separately may well be revealing! This will also give you an idea of the areas you can complement and compensate for at school.

10 **Send portable or pocketbook computers home.** Experience in the inner city suggests that the equipment will be well used and well looked after. It may even be worth considering investing in some pocketbooks or cheap portables for basic writing and keyboard skills. If this is done at home, you can concentrate on developing the content of the writing at school.

11 **Be careful not to disadvantage any children.** It's not their fault if they can't have access to their own machine at home, or if there is no interest in their ICT work there. Try to make it up to them, by arranging for their access at school to be easier or more extended.

Appendix 1 Jargon busting ICT terms for education

Or... 'It's all geek to me!'

Most computing terms are deliberately chosen so as to be confusing to the uninitiated. Either their normal everyday meaning refers to something else entirely, or a deliberately archaic word is used in a new and still more unusual way. It is all part of the 'geek-speak' of the computer world. Learning all of these nerd-words is clearly neither necessary nor helpful, unless you particularly wish to develop some anorak camouflage. The words and terms below are current educational technology jargon. We have offered what we hope is a helpful definition. Most of them are serious.

Words in *italics* are mostly defined in the relevant alphabetical place in the list.

address	The identification of a specific physical or *virtual* place in a network. On the Internet, this address is called a *URL* (Universal Resource Locator). For instance: http://www.ncl.ac.uk is the address for Newcastle University. An e-mail address contains the '@' symbol, eg, s.e.higgins@ncl.ac.uk is the address of one of the authors.
adventure program	A program which usually puts the player or *user* in an imaginary situation. The player is required to take decisions to control the way the adventure progresses. One of the early educational adventure programs was 'Granny's Garden' (produced by 4mation), a current example would be the 'Logical Journey of the Zoombinis' (Brøderbund).
application	A computer program which is specifically designed for a particular purpose (eg, a word processor is an application which handles text).
ASCII	American Standard Code for Information Interchange. This is an agreed standard code for letters, numbers and control codes; it is understood by most computers in the same way that American English is understood by other English speakers – or English English is understood by Americans: only imperfectly!

AUP	Acceptable Use Policy. An agreement which explains the rules of Internet use for an institution. Schools will need such an agreement, both to have clear guidelines for pupils to use and so that parents and governors understand how access to the Internet is managed.
bandwidth	A nerd-word used to describe how much data you can send through a connection to the Net. The greater the bandwidth, the faster the rate of transmission. You can think of it as the information carrying capacity of a connection.
baud rate	Geek-speak for the speed of a *modem* (measured in bits per second). It is interesting that the computer world is as obsessed by capacity and speed as car fanatics or train spotters. 56Kbps (kilobits/sec) is currently a fast speed.
bit	An abbreviation for BInary digiT. It is the basic unit of information in the computer world. A bit is binary number and has one of two values, 0 or 1. Computers can only count to 1 as they have no fingers.
browser	Software that allows people to access and navigate the *World Wide Web*. Most Web browsers, such as Mosaic, *Netscape* or Internet Explorer, are graphical and use text and pictures (and even sound or video). A few are only text-based, such as Lynx. As with most things in the computer world, you never have the latest version which lets you hear the latest whistles and bells.
bug	An error in a computer program which may cause the computer to 'crash' or behave in an otherwise inexplicable manner. Of course, if the computer's behaviour is usually inexplicable it can be difficult to tell.
byte	A single computer character, generally eight *bits*. Each letter displayed on a computer screen occupies one byte of computer memory. 1000 bytes, 1 kilobyte (k), 1000 k = 1 megabyte (Mb), 1000 Mb = 1 gigabyte (Gb)
CAI	Computer Aided (or Assisted) Instruction
CAL	Computer Aided (or Assisted) Learning

CBL	Computer Based Learning. All of these neat acronyms obscure the fact that the computer is only a tool or a medium to present learning material, albeit in a sophisticated way. Teaching, however, is not the same as learning, a fact all teachers know well. You can lead a pupil to computer aided learning...
CD-ROM drive	A form of disk drive which stores information on optical or compact disks. A CD-*ROM* drive is used for getting the information from the disk but cannot usually be used for writing or storing information (although now recordable CDs are becoming available, too).
CD-ROM	Compact Disc-Read Only Memory. A record-like storage medium that uses digital and optical laser technology to store up to about 600 Mb of text, pictures, and sound on a single disk. With newer versions (CD-ROMXA, CDTV, CD-i) animation and video clips can be stored on the disks.
clip art	A file of pictures specifically prepared for use in other files. Clip-art files contain graphic images (geek-speak for pictures).
commercial on-line services	A company which charges people to dial in via a modem to get access to its information and services, which can include the Internet. See also *Internet Service Provider*.
concept keyboard	An input device (geek-alert!) comprising a tablet (A4- or A3-sized) connected to the computer on which overlays can be placed. By pressing different areas of the tablet, actions can be made to happen on the computer (sounds; letters, words, phrases of text; pictures; animations; the control of output devices such as a turtle or robot).
content-free software	Open-ended programs which permit more control of the computer by the user. A word processor, database and spreadsheet are all 'content-free' in that the person using it decides what the content of the file will be. By contrast a 'drill and practice' program has predetermined content.
control	A computer can be made to control a device to which it is connected, such as a disk drive, a printer, a model or robot. The means by which a computer directs a device is often called control technology.
copy	An editing term: the duplication of an item (text, image, sound) to be subsequently *pasted* elsewhere in the same document or transferred to another file.

cursor	The flashing mark which appears on the screen to show where text will appear when a key is pressed on the keyboard. A cursor's shape can be changed. Depending on its shape, a cursor is also called an I bar, a caret, an insertion point, or a mouse pointer! If all else fails try cursing the cursor... it is guaranteed not to work, but may make you feel better.
cut	Another editing term: to remove an item (text, image, sound), which can then be *pasted* elsewhere in the same document or file or transferred to another file.
data	The 'raw' information which a computer handles. Data can take the form of text, numbers or pictures. If your first thought was Commander Data, from Star Trek NG, award yourself two extra nerd points...
data logging	A means by which a computer monitors and records events. For example, a computer can be set up to record the temperature in a room at hourly intervals and then 'log' the data over a period of a week. Sorry, no lumberjacks, OK?
database	A computer application enabling information to be stored, retrieved and manipulated. The most common form of database is the 'flat file', which is like a card index system in structure. There are also many information databases now available on the Internet for searching.
desktop publishing	An application for designing and producing documents that may include text, borders, headings and pictures.
dialogue box	A window which appears on screen giving information which requires a response. In fact no dialogue is possible. You are usually forced to do what the computer requires, a bit like a consultation document in the education world.
Dialup Internet connection	Lets a user dial into an Internet service provider using modem and telephone line to access the Internet. (See also *SLIP or PPP* connections.)
digital camera	A camera that captures an image and stores it in electronic form, which can be downloaded directly into a computer without the need for film. Despite the derivation this has nothing to do with fingers.
digitizer	Geek-alert! A piece of software which transforms a video signal into a digital signal that can be manipulated by the computer. A nerd-word.

dip switch	A small switch (normally in a bank of eight or more) usually found on a printer. Setting the dip switches to different positions controls the way the printer behaves. So called because when nimble little fingers change the position of the switches it makes the printer (and often the teacher) dippier than before.
directory	A collection of files is stored in a directory. A directory is usually given a name to help to identify the files it contains; eg, 'My files' for your files. On-line directories are lists of files or other directories on a computer at an Internet site.
disk drive	A device used for storing computer information on magnetic or optical disks. Schools make use of floppy, hard and optical (CD-ROM) disk drives, some may even have Zip and Jaz drives.
domain name	The part of the Internet address that specifies your computer's location in the world. The address is written as a series of names separated by full stops. The most common top level domains: .ac academic (UK higher education) .edu education (US) .com commercial (US) .co company (UK) .gov governmental or public .mil military .net network resource So (http://www.ncl.ac.uk/) is a website (http://www) for Newcastle (ncl) University (ac) in the UK.
download	The term describing the transfer of information from one computer to another (such as through a modem or from an Internet site). To upload is to send a file to another computer.
drill and practice	Low-level educational programs which are designed to provide instruction or practice with specific skills (eg, spelling, addition).
e-mail	A means of sending (usually) plain text messages between two computers connected via a network.
emoticons	'Smileys' used in e-mail messages to add emotional emphasis: :) for happy ;) for a (knowing) wink :(for sad – turn the page sideways if you don't see why these symbols are used. Part of the geek language.

error message	A message which the computer sends you to inform you that there is a problem, often caused by a *bug,* and displayed immediately prior to a system *crash.* However it is usually *not* you who has made the mistake. These are almost always bad news!
export	To transfer information from one application to another. Typically, if you export something you will probably not use a *port.* Please remember if an export fails, try a Newcastle Brown instead. (A local tip, for inhabitants of north-east England.)
FAQ	Frequently Asked Questions. Files on the Net which store the answers to common questions. If you are stuck, check the FAQs first, before you ask your own question. The following ftp site is useful and holds most FAQ on the Net. Ftp to: rtfm.mit.edu Go to the sub-directory pub/usenet/news.answers
file	Information that is stored, usually in a *folder* or *directory* on a disk. A file is usually given a name to help to identify it. Most pupils build up a collection of files either called by their name Steve1, Steve2, Steve3, or 'untitled'. These names are, therefore, almost completely indistinguishable and it means much time can be fruitlessly spent in locating previously saved work.
filter	Hardware or software designed to restrict access to certain areas on the Internet.
flame	To send a sharp, critical or downright rude e-mail message to another person.
floppy disk	A form of disk used for storing information in electronic form. The plastic case contains a disk of magnetic material, similar to that used in audio and video recorders. Floppy disks store a maximum of 1.6 kilobytes of information. Cunningly, a floppy disk has a hard plastic cover so that it appears neither floppy nor disk-shaped.
FTP	Geek-alert! File Transfer Protocol. An application program that uses TCP/IP protocol to allow you to move files from a distant computer to a local computer, using a network like the Internet. Non-geeks use sensible computers and programs which mean they can avoid the technical details.

function key	A key (usually labelled F0, Fl, F2, etc) which is used by an application to perform a particular task (eg, printing or saving a document). However, in most programs they serve no function or you can't remember which action they are supposed to perform.
gigabyte	See *byte*, or if you don't want the detail, it's bigger than a megabyte, a thousand megabytes in fact.
graphics program	An application which enables the user to create or manipulate images on screen. However sophisticated it is, it will *not* draw graphs.
GUI	Graphical User Interface. Software designed to allow the user to execute commands by pointing and clicking on icons or text. It is nerdily pronounced 'Gooey'. See also WIMP.
hard disk	Most modern computers have internal hard disk drives. Like a floppy disk, a hard disk holds larger amounts of information.
hardware	Computer devices such as the computer itself, the printer, the monitor, the keyboard and mouse – the 'kit'.
highlight	Marking an area of the screen, usually for editing. Most applications show highlighted areas in reverse colours (eg, white on black rather than black on white).
home page	The first page you see when visiting a World Wide Web site.
HTML	Hypertext Mark-up Language. The programming language of the World Wide Web, HTML software turns a document into a hyperlinked World Wide Web page.
HTTP	Hypertext Transfer Protocol. The protocol used to provide hypertext links between pages. It is the standard way of transferring HTML documents between web servers and browsers. Hence why most web addresses start http://
Hypertext/hyperlink	A highlighted word or graphic in a document that, when clicked on, enables you to see the related piece of information from elsewhere on the Internet.
icon	A small picture (or graphic) that can be selected with the mouse pointer and which visually represents a program or file. Most computers now use icons as part of the way you interact with it. (See also *WIMP*.)

ICT	Information and Communications Technologies, used to be just IT (*information technology*).
ILS	Integrated Learning Systems: complex (and expensive) programs offering sophisticated drill and practice for pupils and detailed feedback for teachers.
import	See *export*.
Infobot (or mailbot)	An e-mail address that automatically returns information requested by the user.
Information Superhighway	Originally an American idea, the official US government name for the Internet and other computer networks was the National Information Infrastructure, but it is more commonly known as the Information Superhighway.
information technology	Electronic means for storing, changing and transmitting information.
input device	A piece of equipment for entering information into a computer. A keyboard is an input device for entering text into the computer. Nerd-word.
interface	A device for connecting equipment to a computer. A modem is a form of interface, as it connects the computer to a telephone line.
Internet	No, not World Cup '98 or '02, but the global network linking millions of computers around the world. These computers are called hosts, which our dictionary defines as 'an organism on which another lives as a parasite'. Geek-speak would probably define it more as a sort of virtual space in which users can send and receive e-mail, log-in to remote computers (telnet), browse databases of information in text or hypertext format (gopher, World Wide Web, WAIS), and send and receive programs (ftp) contained on these computers.
Internet account	Purchased through an Internet service provider, the account assigns a password and e-mail address to an individual or group.
Internet server	A computer that stores data that can be accessed via the Internet.

Internet Service Provider (ISP)	Internet Service Provider. Any organization that provides access to the Internet. Many ISPs also offer technical assistance to schools looking at becoming Internet information providers by placing their school's information on-line. They also help schools get connected to the Net.
Internet site	A computer connected to the Internet containing information that can be accessed using an Internet navigation tool such as ftp, telnet, gopher or a web browser.
Intranet	A local network, for example, within a school or cluster of schools.
IP address	Every computer on the Internet has a unique numerical IP address which will look something like 123.45.678.9.
IRC	Internet Relay Chat. Interactive, real-time discussions between people using text messages. People log into designated Net computers and join discussions already in progress. Some IRC channels even discuss nice things!
joystick	An input device which allows control of objects or images on the screen through the movement of a lever, most often used for computer 'arcade' games.
justification	The manipulation of text on a line in a word processor. 'Right justify' aligns all lines to end against the right-hand margin, 'Left justify' aligns the beginning of lines to the left-hand side of the screen, and 'Fully justified' inserts additional gaps between words to begin and end in line with both margins.
keyword	A word or words which can be searched for in documents or menus.
kilobyte (k)	See *byte*.
LAN	Local Area Network: a restricted network, which connects computers within a building or among buildings, for the purpose of sharing voice, data, fax, and/or video. In some parts of the country, schools and LEAs are creating LANs.
laptop computer	See *portable computer*.

LCD screen	Liquid Crystal Display screen: a thin form of monitor screen (about the thickness of two pieces of glass). Electrical charges cause different areas of the screen to change colour. Most calculators use LCD display to show the numbers.
load	To transfer information from a storage device (such as a disk drive) into the computer's memory.
LOGO	A computer programming language whereby instructions are written to control the actions of the computer. LOGO was written by Seymour Papert (among others) to provide a 'low floor, high ceiling' approach to programming – easy enough for infants to use, potentially complex enough to challenge graduates. Professor Seymour Papert now, confusingly, holds the Lego chair!
log on	To sign on to a computer system.
mailing lists (or mailbases)	There are more than 4000 topic-related, e-mail-based message bases that can be read and posted to. People subscribe to the lists they want to read and receive messages from via e-mail. Mailing lists are operated using automatic mailbase (or listserv in the US) software. Thus, many users call mailing lists 'mailbases'. There are two types of lists: moderated and unmoderated. Moderated lists are screened by a person before messages are posted to subscribers. Messages to unmoderated lists are automatically forwarded to subscribers. 'UK-schools' and 'SENCO forum' are examples of mailing lists for teachers.
megabyte (Mb)	See *byte*.
menu	A list of options which can be revealed and then selected by the mouse. Like most menus, they never quite seem to have what you want.
menu bar	A section of the screen (across the top with PC and Macintosh computers, across the bottom of the screen with Acorn computers) on which menus or the icons of applications are placed. None so far serve alcohol.
merge	To bring two different pieces of information together in the same document or file. For example, addresses from a database can be merged with a letter in some word processors to personalize a mailing: hence 'mail-merge'. Geek-speak.

MIDI	Musical Instrument Digital Interface – a system (set of agreed guidelines to ensure conformity) for connecting musical instruments to computers. Quite why trumpets might want to browse the Internet we have not yet discovered.
model	A representation of a situation which enables predictions to be made. Mathematics is used to model reality (eg, when three objects are placed with four objects, there will be seven objects altogether; the model for this is $3 + 4 = 7$). A computer uses mathematical patterns and algorithms to model quite complex situations (eg, global weather patterns, and gets these wrong, too).
modem	An electronic device which connects a computer to a telephone line enabling information to be transferred between computers. A modem is required for connection to the Internet. Fax modems enable faxes to be sent and received by a computer. It is an unhelpful abbreviation for MOdulate DEModulate. Modems are available for any computer, can be internal or external, and come in several speeds, known as the *baud* rate. The higher the baud rate, the faster the modem.
monitor	Just another word for the thing with the screen showing you what the computer is doing: an output device.
mouse	A small plastic box which sits on the table beside a computer and is connected to it or the keyboard by a wire 'tail'. By moving the mouse and pressing its one, two or three buttons, the computer can be controlled. You can now also get tailless mice which use infrared to send signals to the computer. On laptops a variety of trackball, trackpads and what look like little bits of chewing gum are all designed to confuse the uninitiated. Geek-speak plural 'mouses'. Anorak definition: a computer input device.
mouse pointer	See *cursor*.
multimedia	An application which makes use of more than one medium eg, words, pictures and noise. Easier than it sounds.
net surfer	Someone who browses the Internet with no definite destination. Now widely regarded as ancient geek.

netiquette	A geek dialect. The rules of conduct for Internet users. Violating netiquette may result in *flaming* or removal from a *mailing* list. Some service providers (*ISPs*) will even cancel a user's Internet account, thus denying him or her access to the Net, if the violation is severe enough. A fitting punishment indeed!
Netscape	Internet navigation software that allows users to access information through a graphical, point-and-click interface rather than text-only screens or menus. Netscape is known as a web *browser* because it accesses World Wide Web information formatted into special home pages using hypertext. It is free to educational users. Other graphical web browsers include Microsoft's Internet Explorer, Mosaic and Opera.
network	A system linking computers. A local network links computers on the same site (eg, within a school, see LAN). The Internet is a global network.
OILS	Open Integrated Learning Systems: even more complex (and still more expensive) programs than *ILS*, offering still further sophisticated drill and practice for pupils, and detailed feedback for teachers, with more flexibility than basic ILS.
on-line/off-line	When you are logged onto a computer through your modem or a via a network, you are said to be on-line. When you are using your computer, but are not connected to a computer through your modem, you're said to be working off-line. When teaching with WWW materials you might want to *download* them so pupils can use them *off-line*.
operating system	The internal software which controls the way a computer operates. No matter how new your computer is, you never have the latest version. Technical helplines always ask you which version you have and will reply (with the customary sucking in of breath over the teeth) 'Well, if you'd upgraded to version 9.7.1 you would not have had this problem…'
output device	A piece of hardware which enables the computer to represent data for users. A printer is an example of an output device.
palmtop computer	See *portable computer*.

paste	An editing term meaning to place a previously *copied* or *cut* item in a file or document. An unusually appropriate term as many children can get into as much of a mess with cut and paste on a computer as with scissors and glue. Of course, it is harder for them to damage and daub glue on their clothes when cutting and pasting on a computer. Also fewer parents are likely to claim for damage to clothes.
peripheral	A piece of equipment connected to the computer by a cable or wire. Most printers are peripheral devices; they are separately plugged into the computer. A scanner or external hard drive are also types of peripherals. (It is tempting to call them 'ephemerals' because they only work properly when you don't need them to work urgently, and you can never pin down why.)
photo CD	A CD on which photographic images are stored. An ordinary colour film can be processed by most high street chemists into a photo CD (for a small extra charge), enabling photographs to be *imported* directly into the computer.
pirate software	Software which has been illegally copied and used on a computer. Tempting and easy to do in most cases, but illegal. Make sure you have the appropriate licence for the software you use.
pocket computer	See *portable computer*.
podule	An electronic circuit board which is plugged inside a computer to extend its capabilities. Geek-speak.
pointer	See *cursor*.
port	A socket on a computer to plug something into.
portable computer	A small computer. A laptop computer is about the size of a small attaché case. A palmtop or pocket computer is about the size of an adult's hand.
posts	E-mail messages sent to a mailing list or Usenet newsgroup to be read by subscribers or others on the Internet. Nerd-word.
printer	Dot matrix printers are cheap, but are noisy and produce a poor image; ink-jets and bubble-jets are relatively cheap, but use water-based inks; laser jets provide high quality images, but are more expensive.

program	A list of instructions to control the operation of a computer; the term is also used as a verb, 'to program' meaning to create such as a list of instructions.
programmable turtle	A device which children can program to move by carrying out a series of instructions, this could be either just on the screen, or making a robot move across the floor.
programming language	A particular vocabulary and syntax of instructions that can be used to give instructions to a computer.
RAM	Random Access Memory: part of a computer's memory, which is used for storing loaded programs and files; the easiest analogy is that it is the computer's working, thinking or operating memory.
ROM	Read Only Memory: part of the computer's memory, which contains fixed information, such as the computer's operating system. Also used for a CD-ROM as the disk can only be read and not written to.
save	To transfer information from the computer's operating memory to a storage device such as a disk drive.
scanner	A flatbed scanner looks like a photocopier; takes a picture of what is being scanned and turns it into digital information so that it can appear and be used by a computer. A hand-held scanner is a smaller device, which performs the same function, but it is 'swiped' across a piece of paper-based information.
sensor	A device that a computer can use to monitor external events, such as temperature or light levels.
shareware	Software which does not have to be paid for until it is used. Shareware can be downloaded from the Internet. Most shareware authors deny that they ever receive *any* money. This is either because anorakish users are too mean to pay for something someone was foolish enough to make available free, or is a good tax dodge. Most shareware programs are excellent, some may have unexpected results like a *virus*.
signature file	Return address information such as name, telephone number, and e-mail address that is automatically put at the bottom of e-mail messages to save retyping basic information.

simulation	A computer model of a situation: the user can enter information into the simulation and the computer will respond with an appropriate outcome. Simulations make it possible to model parts of expensive, difficult, complex, hazardous or impossible situations. However, like most complex things that are simulated, there is always something missing.
SLIP or PPP	Serial Line Internet Protocol (SLIP) or Point to Point Protocol (PPP) Internet connections. Both allow a computer to connect to the Internet using a modem and telephone line. Users then navigate the Internet using software on their own computer. This is in contrast to using a Dialup Internet Connection, where a user is forced to navigate the Net using a text-based set of menus.
software	The programs (or procedures) used to instruct the computer.
sort	To put items into order (alphabetical or numerical). This process is often used by databases and spreadsheets. Some word processors allow paragraphs and lists to be sorted alphabetically.
spam	Slang for posting the same message to multiple newsgroups – frowned on by most people on the Internet.
speech	See *voice synthesis*.
spreadsheet	A computer application that resembles a large grid of cells. Each cell can be linked to any other by a formula. If information is changed in one cell, all other interlinked cells are changed according to the linking formulae. As might be predicted, you cannot spread it straight from the 'fridge' but it will print out on lots of sheets of paper.
stress sensor	All modern technical equipment has a hidden stress sensor. The more stressed you are, or the more anxious you become, the more likely the stress sensor will leap into action. On a computer this means that it will perform mundane tasks in a new and creative way, wiping half of your word-processing file as you print it out, for example. Every school's office photocopier has one attached to the green 'start' button, which ensures a major breakdown the day before all the school's paperwork has to be sent to OFSTED.

system software	See *operating system*.
Telnet	Allows people to access computers and their data at thousands of places around the world, most often at libraries, universities, and government agencies. Text-based, but relatively fast.
trackerball	An input device which controls the mouse pointer by means of a large ball mounted in a cradle – similar in action to an upturned (or dead) mouse. Can be particularly useful for pupils with limited fine motor skills.
turtle	See *programmable turtle*.
upload	To send information to another computer or network.
Usenet newsgroups	More than 17 000 topic-oriented message bases that can be read and posted to. Also called newsgroups.
user	One who uses a computer. However, to most normal people the word clearly has anorakish and addictive connotations.
user group	A group of like-minded people who have a similar interest. User groups communicate by e-mail. See also *user*.
VDU	Visual Display Unit – see *monitor*.
VGA	Video Graphics Array – a standard which specifies the way computers communicate with monitors to ensure conformity.
virtual	A much overused term implying something is not quite real. A computer-generated environment.
virus	A computer virus is a cunning and occasionally malicious little program which 'infects' a computer's files or operating system. Some viruses can damage a computer by, for example, altering or deleting the contents of files. Viruses are often transferred from one computer to another by floppy disks or over the Internet. All hard-drive-based machines should have some virus protection software installed. It is depressing to consider that they have been created by talented individuals with nothing better to offer the computing community than a widget which weasels its way into your computer and damages it.

voice input	Some computers can be controlled by voice. There are also several software programs that can learn to recognize an individual's voice so you can dictate and have your words appear on screen.
voice synthesis	A software application which almost, but not quite, unsuccessfully simulates the sound of the human voice. It usually comprises a series of phonemes (phonetic sounds) which are strung together by the computer to form sounds which are almost, but not quite, unlike words. A more accurate description would be a synthetic voice, perhaps polyester or rayon.
WIMP	*Windows*, Icons, Menus, Pointers – the environment that is used to interact with most mouse-controlled computers. You move the mouse and point and click. A *GUI interface* is operated through a WIMP environment. There! You can now read geek!
window	A framed area of the computer screen. Several windows can be displayed on the screen. Usually only one window is 'active' at any one time and is able to be used. So called because you cannot see through them. They rarely shed any light on the situation and the one you actually want to see is hidden by all the others.
word processor	An *application* for displaying and manipulating text. Unfortunately computers are not yet able to produce appropriate words to process.
World Wide Web (WWW)	Part of the Internet which communicates information in text, images, sounds and animation using 'hypertext'. By moving the mouse over parts of a World Wide Web page and clicking a button, you are given more information or are transferred to other web 'sites'. Also known as the 'World Wide Wait' because of long download times over telephone lines.
zoom	To magnify part of an image for more detailed work, or to reduce the size of an image to see more of it on screen. Often shown as a percentage of the full size. Zooming to 200 per cent increases the area to four times the original (2 times 2). When interviewed, most teachers claimed to prefer Strawberry Mivvis.

Appendix 2   Audit your own ICT skills with quick quiz!

A.

Please mark the boxes that *best* describe your skills in relation to the types of computers and the computing terms below:

	2	1	0	–1	Score

Types of computers and operating systems

	2	1	0	–1	Score
BBC 'B' Master	Can load and run programs	Can turn it on	Don't know where the switch is	I prefer looking for Channel 5	
Acorn series	Use regularly and can even save and print files!	I have had a go	I would really rather not	Acorns are for squirrels	
PC/DOS Windows	Regular user	Used a bit	Never tried	I keep the curtains shut	
RM/Nimbus	Confident with Window Box/RM applications	Had a try	Seen in school	Are they the ones that mean it will rain?	
Apple Mac	Don't like to use anything else	Fiddled with one once	They look quite nice	Are they the red crunchy ones?	

	2	1	0	−1	Score

Types of applications

	2	1	0	−1	Score
Word processing	Confident	Use a bit	Will have to learn soon	I prefer a biro	
Spreadsheets	Confident	Beginner	Never used	I prefer a duvet	
CD-ROM	Happy to use	Had a play	Seen demonstrated	You can't beat the old LPs	
Hard drive	Know about	Can use	Heard of	Some sort of car rally?	
Floppy disk	Know about	Got some somewhere	I think I've seen one	Prefer an osteopath	
Concept keyboard	Can make overlays	Watched pupils using one	Heard of	A what?	
Clip art	Have done DTP	Printed a picture out once	Friend mentioned it	An Aussie sheep shearing award?	
Scanners	Can scan pictures and do OCR on text	Watched pupils using one	Seen one	Good film, wasn't it?	
E-mail	Have my own @ address	Have used	Heard of	Couldn't get the stamp on	
World Wide Web	Often go surfing	Looked at a few pages	Saw something about it once	Don't like Spiderman	
The Internet	Use e-mail, web searches, Telnet, etc confidently	Had a play	Seen the media hype	Spanish trawlers should stay OUT of British waters!	

B.

Please circle a number to show how you feel about computers on the scale below:

(1 = hate them : 6 = love them)

1	2	3	4	5	6	

C.

Do you use a computer for your work at home?   **Yes/No**

Total

Scoring:	Section A – Score 2, 1 ,0 or –1 according to the grid Section B – Use the score from the rating scale Section C – Yes 2, No 0
Totals:	
40	Consider buying a new anorak. You have little to learn from the information revolution and will keep yourself up to date with new technology regardless of the personal and social consequences.
30–39	Not a lot you can learn either, the main challenge is now using the equipment effectively with your pupils.
20–29	You clearly have a range of strengths and weaknesses, but are well on the way to grappling with the challenge that ICT poses for teachers.
10–19	A few gaps in your knowledge that you perhaps ought to consider addressing. Time to nag the head for some new equipment as well.
0–9	It must be difficult to meet the demands of the National Curriculum! You ought to consider updating your knowledge and skills. Soon.
Below 0	Either sheer dedication has kept you in blissful ignorance of the current communications revolution or you simply liked the humour! The latter could perhaps be excused…

Appendix 3   Top 20 web sites

This list will never stay up to date. The web is evolving rapidly, particularly in the area of education. We have tried to suggest sites that we think will be around for the next few years. It also reflects our personal interests. There will be hundreds of other sites we could have listed. In addition the last link will take you to a *500 Tips for ICT* web page which we will try to keep updated with information. There are links for teachers (have you seen your school's OFSTED report on-line?), suggestions for links to support different areas of the curriculum, and sites designed particularly for children. We have tried to give a brief flavour of what is available…

http://www.ngfl.gov.uk/ The National Grid for Learning. Need we say more? You've read the hype now have a look.

http://www.vtcentre.com/index.html The Virtual Teacher's Centre, sponsored by BT, Microsoft and RM. Being a little pedantic, we wonder if it is a virtual centre for teachers or a centre of virtual teachers…

http://www.open.gov.uk/dfee/ The official government web site with on-line copies of most new documents. School performance tables and the National Curriculum are available here, too! (http://open.gov.uk/dfee/perform/title.htm and http://www.dfee.gov.uk/nc/)

http://www.ofsted.gov.uk/ OFSTED's site with inspection reports, press releases and HMCI reports.

http://www.crownbc.com/qca/menu.htm The Qualifications and Curriculum Authority (QCA).

http://www.becta.org.uk/ British Educational Communications and Technology agency (BECTa), formerly National Council for Educational Technology (NCET). They have a remit 'to ensure that technology supports the DfEE's objectives to drive up standards, in particular to provide the professional expertise the DfEE needs to support the future development of the National Grid for Learning. BECTa will also have a role in the further education sector's developing use of ICT, in the identification of ICT opportunities for special educational needs, and in the evaluation of new technologies as they come on stream'.

http://www.yahoo.com/Education/ Yahoo's education index. Try K12 and literacy links. Can be a bit frustrating until you find an area you like.

http://members.aol.com/dcrolf/uk-schools/index.htm UK-Schools information. Has a good web guide and information on the UK-schools e-mail discussion list.

http://www.tes.co.uk:8484/tp/9013541/PRN/teshome.html The on-line version of *The Times Educational Supplement.*

http://www.mathworld-interactive.com/ Math World Interactive is a US site 'dedicated to helping educators and parents motivate their students to solve open-ended word problems, communicate mathematically, and share cultural and geographical information.' New problems are posted every nine weeks for different age groups.

http://www.shareware.com/ An index of *some* of the shareware (cheap or free programs) available on the Internet. There is an education section and you can search for particular platforms or operating systems.

http://www.campus.bt.com/CampusWorld/ BT's Campus world with sections for teachers and schools wanting to use the Internet more.

http://www.eduweb.co.uk/ RM's Internet site for schools.

http://schools.channel4.com/ Channel 4's web site.

http://ed.info.apple.com/education/index.html Apple's Education site has good tips for using programs like Claris Works.

http://web66.umn.edu/ Web 66 An American site, but has good links about education. 'Just as US Highway Route 66 was a catalyst for Americana, we see the World Wide Web as a catalyst that will integrate the Internet into K12 school curricula. The Web66 project is designed to facilitate the introduction of this technology into K12 schools.'

http://www.ipl.org/ref/ The Internet public library reference centre.
http://sunsite.berkeley.edu/KidsClick!/ Kids Click – a children's web searching point based at Berkeley in California, but not bad for grown ups either!

http://www.netskills.ac.uk/TONIC/ The On-Line Internet Course based at Newcastle University: 'the course provides an introduction to the Internet and computer networks in general, describing and illustrating the main software tools for navigating the networks. However, these tools are only a means to an end, the end being the wealth of information and communication resources offered via the networks. The course looks at types and examples of networked information, at the means for searching that information, and at the communication facilities and resources on the net'.

http://searchenginewatch.com/ The Search Engine Watch Information about searching on the web, how search engines work, good sites for children, etc.

http://www.staff.ncl.ac.uk/s.e.higgins/500 tips/ A site designed to help maintain up-to-date references that build upon the links suggested here, and a forum for comment about the book.

Appendix 4   Starting points for software

Your local LEA IT centre should have programs you can look at, and may well have offers that are cheaper than you, as an individual school, can buy them from suppliers. The contacts below are ones we have ourselves found useful.

TAG Developments Ltd, 25 Pelham Road, Gravesend, Kent, DA11 0HU
E-mail: info@tagdev.co.uk
Tel: 01474 357350
Fax: 01474 357887
http://www.tagdev.co.uk/
TAG has a good catalogue and a range of software and hardware for primary schools.

SEMERC
1 Broadbent Road, Watersheddings, Oldham OL1 4LB
Tel: 0161 627 4469
Fax: 0161 627 2381
E-mail: info@semerc.demon.co.uk
http://www.semerc.com/
SEMERC is also a good place to start for UK primary schools and offers a range of software, particularly for SEN.

BECTa web site and CD reviews at:
http//www.becta.org.uk

Companies

Sherston Software, well known in most primary schools...
They accept orders by phone 01666 840433, fax 01666 840048 or by e-mail sales@sherston.co.uk or from their web site http://www.sherston.com/

Software on the web...

In addition to the specific sites listed above, try Tony Pickford's (Chester College) pages, he has a good links page for software for primary teachers at:
http://www.geocities.com/Athens/5732/edsoft.html

A good place to start on the web for more general browsing about educational software is:
http://www.microweb.com/pepsite/Software/publishers.html
which lists nearly 2000 educational software web sites for parents or
http://www.educ.sfu.ca/cet/EduResources/CET_Software.html
which is San Francisco University's Educational Technology site; however both of these sites are American...

Appendix 5   Some British educational acronyms and abbreviations

('Ed' speak?)

Frequently in this book we refer to documents, procedures, governmental organizations and various kinds of personnel by their acronyms or abbreviated versions of their proper titles. Readers, who are teachers based in England and Wales, will be familiar (maybe all too familiar!) with this terminology. Even as close as Scotland and Northern Ireland there are significant differences, and for readers in different parts of the world some of the jargon could be impenetrable without some help (even though there are likely to be similar systems and terms under different names). For anyone to whom these terms are not clear, and for those who might enjoy a wry smile at the expense of some familiar friends, we offer a brief, and perhaps only slightly jaundiced 'translation' of them below.

- **Attainment Targets, or ATs.** Statements that describe where every child should be, in terms of their educational development, by the end of each Key Stage.

- **Department for Education and Employment, or DfEE.** The closest thing there is to an educational deity in England and Wales. Many teachers are beginning to wonder whether burnt offerings or sacrifices are required to appease the great DfEE spirit to help it to stop changing its mind all the time.

- **Grant Maintained.** A system introduced under the Conservative government 1993– 1997 whereby a school had all of its budget handed over to use however it saw fit (previously a significant proportion of each school's budget had been controlled by its Education Authority). Suspicions about this apparently rather sensible notion were raised simply because the   Government of the day seemed to think it was *such* a good idea.

- **Individual Education Programme, or IEP.** Many children identified as having special educational needs have an education programme written from them, setting out how identified issues will be tackled. Often these are agreed between the class teacher, the special needs coordinator and the child's parents.

- **In-Service Training, or INSET.** The process by which qualified teachers have their skills updated and enhanced by highly trained educators, coordinators or advisers, theoretically! In practice, a bit of a lottery really.

- **Key Stages, or KS.** In England and Wales, children who have not yet reached compulsory school age (the term in which they turn five) but are attending mainstream school are considered to be in the *'Early Years'*. Children *in* mainstream school between the ages of five and the year in which they turn seven are in *Key Stage 1* (usually from Reception to Year 2), and those between seven and eleven are in *Key Stage 2* (usually Year 3 to Year 6). It is amazing how many complications such an apparently simple system can produce, although the children seem to tune in to it without much difficulty!

- **Local Education Authority, or LEA.** Basically just the section of the local council that is responsible for all public sector, educational establishments that have avoided Grant Maintained status.

- **Office for Standards in Education, or OFSTED.** The second closest thing there is to an educational deity in the England and Wales. OFSTED are responsible for inspecting schools and advising them on how to improve standards and efficiency. Many teachers are beginning to wonder whether it is their inspectors who should become the burnt offerings sent to the DfEE spirit!

- **Programme of Study, or POS.** Set out in the National Curriculum, and often rewritten in greater detail for use in individual schools. Simply, it sets out what sorts of skills and knowledge should be acquired, and the sorts of experiences and activities the children should have, and roughly when they should have achieved them.

- **Scheme of Work, or SOW.** A more detailed plan that puts flesh on the bones of a Programme of Study.

- **School Improvement Plan, or SIP; School Development Plan, or SDP.** It would be thought that these terms are fairly self-explanatory but, surprisingly, the plans themselves are used with highly varying degrees of success. A plan that sets out a school's goals, and how it is intended to meet these goals – usually over a three-year period – during which time the National Curriculum will be updated, OFSTED's criteria will have been improved twice, three government initiatives will come and go, and the office that deals with assessment and curriculum will have been merged, scaled up, scaled down and renamed. We can't understand why improvement plans seem so difficult to manage.

- **Special Educational Needs, or SEN.** Receiving much more attention now than in the past. The term is used to cover everything from a pupil experiencing a brief period of difficulty in a single, specific area of learning, to extreme learning difficulties. SEN is subject to strict guidelines.

- **Special Needs Coordinator, or SENCO.** The only teacher in school with a job that is even more impossible than the ICT coordinator's! We know of one poor soul who has the dubious honour of holding both posts at once, but who still manages to stay relatively sane.

- **Standard Attainment Test, or SAT.** Compulsory, national tests, currently in English, maths and science, that are supposed to assess attainment at the end of each Key Stage. Recently, pilot tests have been used at more frequent intervals, giving a fair indication as to the direction that formal testing is heading in UK schools!

- **The Qualifications and Curriculum Agency, or QCA.** The bit of government that puts the DfEE's desires into practice. It is responsible for producing assessment materials and processes. It disseminates information about the curriculum and how it should be tackled. Kind of like an enforcer!

- **The Teacher Training Agency, or TTA.** A government organization that generates research and papers on the state of the British education system at a mind-boggling pace. Their apparent objective *is* to try to ensure that all teachers have access to the 'right' kinds of training and the 'right' kinds of resources to help them improve their teaching. What 'right' actually constitutes is still under debate, but that fact doesn't seem to dampen their spirits much.

Appendix 6
Further reading

Bennett, Richard (1997), *Teaching IT, (Part of Teaching at Key Stage 1 Series)*, Nash Pollock Publishing, Oxford, UK.

Byrne, J (1995) *Easy Access for Windows 95*, QUE, Indianapolis, USA.

Cassel, P (1995) *Teach Yourself Access 95*, SAMS, Indianapolis, USA.

Courter, G and Marquis, A (1997) *MS Office 97 (No Experience Required)*, Sybex, California, USA.

Gertler, N (1997) *Using MS PowerPoint 97*, QUE, Indianapolis, USA.

James, Frances and Kerr, Ann (1997) *Creative Computing*, Belair Publications, Twickenham, UK.

Kennedy, J (1995) *UK Comms Information Superhighway*, BSB, St Albans, UK.

Kent, P (1994) *Complete Idiot's Guide to the Internet*, QUE, Indianapolis, USA.

Levine, J et al (1997) *The Internet For Dummies*, IDG Books, Foster City, California, USA.

McDowell, S and Race, P (1998) *500 Computing Tips for Trainers*, Kogan Page, London, UK.

Navarro, A and Khan, T (1998) *Effective Web Page Design*, Sybex, California, USA.

Nelson, S (1995) *Field Guide to PCs*, Microsoft Press, Washington, DC, USA

Packard, E, Packard, N and Brown, S (1997) *500 Tips for Primary Teachers*, Kogan Page, London, UK.

Perry, G (1997) *Teach Yourself Windows 95 in 24 Hours*, SAMS, Indianapolis, USA.

Race, P and McDowell, S (1996) *500 Computing Tips for Teachers and Lecturers*, Kogan Page, London, UK.

Straker, Anita and Govier, Heather *Children Using Computers*, (Second Edition 1997), Nash Pollock Publishing, Oxford, UK.

Index